THE IT REVOLUTION IN
series edited by Ant

16

EDILSTAMPA
editrice dell'ANCE

COVER

A tattoo machine in action - self-inscription on the back
(image from François Roche)

Edilstampa srl
Via Guattani, 24
00161 Roma
tel. 0684567403
fax 0644232981
www.edilstampa.ance.it

Roma, may 2014

Antonino Di Raimo

François Roche
Heretical Machinism and Living Architectures of New-Territories.com

preface by Antonino Saggio

New-Territories.com

Portrait of New-Territories.com

New-Territories is a platform which gather the evolution of the multiple names during this last 20 years: BoyeRoche 89 / Roche* 90 / Roche&François 91 / Roche, François, Lewis, Huber, Roubaud, Perrin 92 / Roche, DSV & Sie 93-97 / R, DSV & Sie .P 98 / R&Sie.D/B:L 99 -2001 / R&Sie... 2001-2004 / R&Sie(n)...2004 to now...+ [eIf/b t/c]...from 2011...R&Sie(n) and its avatar names is an architectural practice based initially on Paris. It was founded initially by François Roche, architect (creation 1993-..., Paris), Stéphanie Lavaux, artist (period 1993-2011, French Réunion island), and Gilles Desevedavy, architect (period 1993-1998), followed by Olivier Legrand, Alexandre Boulin (period 1998-2000), Jean Navarro (period 2000-2007), Kiuchi Toshikatsu (period 2007-2011)...[eIf/b t/c] is a studio of "Contigent Scenario" founded in 2011 by François Roche and Camille Lacadée (1986, Bordeaux), with partnership among the other with the artists Philippe Parreno and Pierre Huyghe..., the architects Benoit Durandin, Francois Perrin, Ammar Eloueni, and on many scenario and design, the robotic designer Stephan Henrich, based in BKK and NYC.

My thoughts and my gratitude to to Prof. Antonino Saggio for having generously offered me this space, which I do not hesitate, for various reasons, to define as vital. I wish to thank the architect François Roche for the willingness he showed towards my requests. The image on the cover is the fruit of his suggestion, originating from a scrupulous reading of the text.
My thanks to Roche for the images presented in this book as well.
A thought to Polis University and to Albania, seeing as it is the place where I finished this book, which was conceived and begun in Rome.
Special thanks go to Pasquale Strazza for his help in the page layout.

Photographical References
All of the photos, the renderings, and the project designs are the property of New-Territories.com.

Translation
English translation by Kalina Yamboliev

Living Architectures: Heresy or Future?

preface by Antonino Saggio

Antonino Di Raimo's book, dedicated to François Roche and to *New-Territories*, the group founded by Roche, raises questions of great importance for the development of architectural research and Information Technology in the coming years. Here they are in brief: What role can new material technologies have in a process in which the same materials have incorporated "within" themselves growing shares of active behavior? For example, will they be self-cleaning, un-polluting, self-changing?
In what measure can these active behaviors be assimilable to those in a "living system," in particular when the elements are "interconnected" and can simulate processes typical of living beings (transpiration, dilation, growth, life and death)?
Can we begin to speak of living "systems" in reference to architecture, having seen that the diction of intelligent builiding (also thanks to Artificial Intelligence and to the great development of sensors and electronic components) can already be considered at least theoretically assimilated?
These questions are fundamental today for a combination of reasons that the work of François Roche raises to the highest level, and which involve more general questions that it may now be the moment to summarize.

The Frame of Reference
The first question of a general character regards the growing role that science and technology should have in engaging with important issues of architecture and of society. The future of metropolitan areas rests primarily on the prospect of a successful organic interweaving of city-planning and architecture with science. This affirmation implies a change in the state of the discipline of city-planning itself, to make it converge towards a science of complexities and interrelations: towards an authentic ecology of space.
Robotics, miniaturization, and the diffusion of communication and transport networks open the opportunity for a "compensation" of historical scale. In areas which have been constructed at high density, or in highly industrialized areas that have now fallen into disuse and

are vacant, it is possible to introduce vegetation, nature, and equipment for the intervening time. New concessions of multi-functional infrastructure could capitalize on technological systems that use discoveries from the environmental sciences to restore, clean, and depollute cities, and to direct energy away from indiscriminate growth and more towards recuperation, densification, and the re-use of enormous areas that have remained abandoned and trapped in existing cities.

A state of hybridization between the natural and artificial drives many sectors of architectural research today. New research increasingly tends towards the creation of a type of a panorama, which is reactive, complex, animated, and alive in a process of combination with technological and environmental elements.

In this process of hybridization, the catalyzing role of Information Technology is key for at least three reasons. First, the information community formulates a comprehensive model of both the city and urban landscape which makes structures and cities increasingly resemble the "multitasking" aspects of calculators with mixed uses, superimposed flux, twenty-four hour open cycles of production, free time, and residential uses. Second, Information Technology produces "mathematic models" to examine the chemical, physical, and biological world, and the geological complexity of nature. These simulation models allow for new relational structures. In this process, technology provides the essential instruments to create, project, and finally to construct the plans and buildings conceived with complex systemic methods. Third, Information Technology endows the architecture of reactive systems in such a way as to simulate natural behavior, not only to evoke rules of formation in a "land form architecture," but also to propose environments that are capable of interacting effectively, and in continuous evolution. In this context, technology enters directly into the very fibers of new buildings, capitalizing on electronic interconnections to create environments that transform into variations of real situations. In this same book series the last two books published, Cesare Griffa's *Smart Creatures* and Elisabetta Bonafede's *Plasma Works*, offer numerous examples. A question emerges from this list of reasons which regards the "constructive" role of IT in this new context. Antonino Di Raimo has rightly placed the concept of information at the start of his text. But why is information considered the raw material of architecture in this historical period?

The great change taking place in these years regards the understanding of a new conception of space. Implicitly the paradigm of the industrial world is tied to Newtonian physics, predicting that objects "positioned" in a three-dimensional space exist, upon which the laws of classical physics are in force.
But the idea held by architects of the new generation overturns these concepts. For them no space exists in which objects and architecture meet, but rather *relations* that together deform and create the concept of space and that of object. Nor are the two disassociated as container and contained, but mold and interweave with one another. In this conception space is not a given but only a variation of the very concept of information, belonging to the sphere of representation and tied to conventional contextual and biological meanings. Architects are beginning to think of molding no longer as a thing that "is" but rather believe that they themselves can create time and space, thanks to telecommunication systems, the internet, virtual reality, the possibility of combining hybrid technological and real systems, and to the possibility of incorporating information into matter itself. Information is not only a manipulable element in this new idea of space and of time but becomes vital "fluid," inserting itself into the cycle of buildings and becoming the nourishment to make them live, flower, decay, and regenerate. Interactive informational systems are not regulated solely by the "mechanical" behaviors of the building, but are tied to its "vital" behaviors. These vital behaviors have elements in common with bioclimatic aspects, with the big theme of sustainability and in a complex network of systems and relations.

Roche's Work
In this context the figure of François Roche is a crucial personality, with the longest militancy both in theory and planning. He has been at the forefront of these themes since the mid 1990's, and has produced a large number of interesting projects, some of which have been recognized as masterpieces and presented as models at the "Non Standard Architecture" exhibit in the Centro Pompidou in Paris. Some of his works have also been published in recent architectural accounts. His continual self-interrogation on the themes that we have delineated opens proposals which are so innovative that they seem provocative.
Roche is bringing attention to systemic architectures, which are active in the environment not only because they take energy from it but also

because they function in various ways as elements of filtration and purification. The particularity of his research consists in it being rooted in specific aspects in the development of digital nature and informatics, and which are not only technological and ecological. Roche works actively on two of the most important fronts of contemporary research, or, if it is preferred, on the two greatest crises that stand before us. On one side is the question of how to orient architectural research within Information Technology toward more substantial, rather than superficial, aspects. On the other is how to approach an architecture which is more informed and sustainable without lowering the level of formal and expressive research, but rather finding new reasons for it.

In effect, Roche and the group New-Territories work first on the symbolic and evocative value of architecture, then on the theme of the landscape and, of course, on architecture's relations with natural phenomena. At the same time Roche has a profound interest in themes of Information Technology research that rest on the slopes of programmability and interactivity. The particularity of his approach is that these themes are combined and reinforced against each other as if they were permeated by an information-natural sap, which orients them towards a new logical and expressive order.

Few architects today engage in the new and varied components of building with systemic logic as Roche does. In the more specifically-formal interpretation of research on themes of landscaping, for example, many architects have worked for years on design-actions such as to interweave, superimpose, entwine, and channel. In these cases the architect still remains a "representation" of morphological actions, whether of natural or vegetal origins. But in the current of Roche's research the actions are truly organic actions: breathe, perspire, transpire, digest. This different departure ends in an important outcome. The structures tend to be by nature living beings. The act of breathing that is at their root, for example, transforms their state into a hybrid and intermediate zone that combines the vegetal essence with the material. It is one thing to simulate the tissue of a tree to create an analogous pattern, another to seek to understand its formative logic, and yet another to have a vegetal wall inserted into a logical and organic system.

In 1998 Roche had already designed the new seat of the Iuav in Venice where, inspired by the lagoon, he made the building function like a large undertow. Then in the Venice Biennale of 2000 the steamboat was becoming a floating bar that purified canal waters. Hybrid Muscle used the force of a large buffalo to produce energy in a small, multifunctional pavilion while the Olzweg project in 1996 was using recycled glass to build an internal addition to the courtyard of a museum. In each of these cases there is always a fundamental condition which Roche calls "hyper-localism." It is a component that, along with others, allows for the organization of a project in an effectively logical, not mechanical, system that can't help but be based on marked local specificities.

The Un-Plug project, a tall building in Paris built in 2001 and commissioned by the electric society, operates on renewable energy (primarily light, wind, and solar energy). The facades, equipped with both solar-receptor panels and light-cell coverings, are reactive membranes. The architecture thus becomes simultaneously a consumer and producer of energy which, in excess, is inserted into the network. Un-Plug, which wants to disconnect itself from urban soil and from the urban electric network, also introduces research that is aimed towards an architecture and urbanism that are no longer tied to fixed networks of distribution (hydric, energetic, of charge) but which are potentially composed of free and self-sufficient "un-plugged" elements precisely. These seem utopian visions but, in reality, with the tremendous technological advances of the last years, and with the arrival of a commercial ladder of nanotechnology, these hypotheses constantly find more space for actualization. Some avant-guard schools around the world, in addition to research groups, are beginning to hold courses aimed at rethinking the methods of teaching architecture on the basis of these new principles.

Roche is in the process of realizing a series of important projects, particularly in Bangkok, Thailand. Toyo Ito waited many years to win the Pritzker Architecture prize, and we celebrate that it has come earlier for Roche. The themes his work inspires for future generations of architects are important not only for the future of the planet, but for how architecture itself can be radically modified from how it is intended today and instead come to play a decisive role in the synthesis of necessity, function, and the magic by which fluid secrets are hidden only in the realm of art.

Di Raimo's book analyzes the decisive aspects of many of Roche's projects with precision and intelligence. The author studies not only the outcomes but also the processes, disassembling the projects to understand them, and thus offering the reader a very useful and interesting text. While Di Raimo analyzes numerous of the issues noted, he emphasizes with alacrity the larger historical question Roche's work poses. He writes:

Critical approaches within the cognitive sciences, linked closely to the development of Computer Science, have placed at the center of their own reflection the limits of a computational approach to cognition. They propose new contributions, such as the idea of the mind as a network, by basing this "connectionism" on the biological model of neural networks, and above all in robotics – the "embodied" – where the mind and thus cognition are never separated from the fact of residing in a body (and not in a computer), or of being situated in an "environment". Consequently the development of related technologies, above all robotics, have evolved in these directions, proposing systems that are increasingly capable of communicating with their environment, and which increasingly configure themselves as ecological networks of relations that do not function like electronic machines separate from the context. In particular, this "embodied" approach is founded on the crucial fact of possessing a body situated in an environment that is by definition ecologic. This approach does not place, at the center of cognitive experience, a simulation of the environment, which is detached on the part of the organism or the artificial agent, but rather the organism itself, and its *psychological, historical, and sensorimotor experience* within that environment.

Ultimately, if an "eco-systemic" approach to architecture is to take place today, architecture must belong simultaneously to the earth (that is, to matter), to the cloud (meaning, to informatics), and to the body (the living body). Such interconnection is the crisis and challenge before us, and François Roche exposes it well. This book will help us to think, perhaps for the first time with clarity, about these issues through the work of one of the greatest among the new architects.

http://www.arc1.uniroma1.it/saggio/it

1. A Critical Position: Reconcilable Dualities Between Machines and Living Entities

Preamble - Aqua Alta in Venice
Along the side of a canal in a historic city, a new architecture appears which seems to contain water. Its silhouette reproduces the three-dimensional imprint of a pre-existing building. The contents are overturned, however, triggering a new and radical relationship for the context. While areas of the floor plan could be recognized as having been conceived as spaces for activities relating to instruction, it turns out that the undulating walls that define them – *the digitalization of waves*, says the architect – are capable of sucking water up from the canal, using the well-known effect of capillary action. From pollutants to living communities, the walls show a world – that of water – that is able not only to replace the vertical structures of an architectural space, but also to make aspects of the situation tangible which are normally ignored. These waved walls are not only able to replace the traditional vertical structures of an architecture space, moreover they are able to show a world – that of the water – making tangible those aspects of the environment which are normally ignored.

Venice: at times polluted, at times pure. Whether in symbiosis or in antagonism with the city, water is a constitutive part of Venice where the local architecture has historically needed to, and must still, negotiate its very existence. The precarious balance between the water that cyclically rises and the city that is slowly sinking becomes not only the catalyst by which an idea is born, but also the most intimate reason for a new and lively architecture. Thus, despite the clear digitization of the wave proposed in the division of spaces here, the value of this project is not in the morphology generated by the computer. Far from any formal speculation the wave does not seem to want to materialize aesthetic and literary dimensions, as is customary in Venice, but rather the ecological constitution of the city and the millenarian negotiations that communities, living or non-living, have had with the site.

Aqua Alta is a project of the French group New-Territories, developed [12] by the International Competition for the expansion of the IUAV (University of Architecture of Venice). We are in 1998 and the French architecture firm led by the architect François Roche already shows clearly, through this proposal, some themes of its own original and heretical design research: science coupled with aesthetics, ecology with politics, and simulation with narration.

THE DIGITALIZATION OF WAVES

*Losing its purely-formal rhetoric, the wave becomes an ecological device of spatial
distribution, of the aspiration of water, and of the creation of a new material for architecture.*

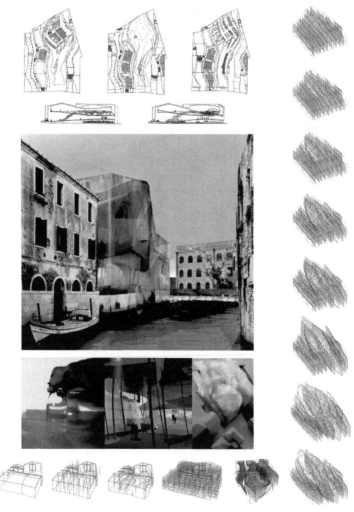

AQUA ALTA, VENICE, 1998
*Plans and sections (top), the elevation along the canal, the concept, the interior, a model
(center), and a generative diagram of the wave (in the right column and in the bottom row).*

1.1 New-Territories.com: New Territories for Heretical Scenarios
New-Territories is the platform that collects all of multiple names, with their respective designations and evolutions, of the groups led by Roche over the last twenty years. It is known in Italy as R&Sie(n) (a name used from 2001 to 2011), the acronym of which is composed of the initials of the members of the group or which is perhaps intended as a play of letters to be read as *heresy*.
New Territories, which will be indicated as N.T. from here on, has created an *other* path with respect to the dominant attitudes in architecture, which is designed within the information paradigm and which has been able to open radically new scenarios that characterize the uniqueness of their research.
Through Roche's philosophical restlessness, N.T. has been able to build a methodology based on the constant expansion of meanings in manipulating information in architectural design processes and production, which even involve the architecture's specific material nature. Far from any linguistic speculation deriving from the processing capacity of computers or from the parameterization of the formal processes, as happened with Peter Eisenman and Zaha Hadid to highlight just two players in the first phase, N.T. probes the conceptual core of the information paradigm. It poses the unprecedented question by which information does not only have a meaning in configuring architecture, but may be its most important organizational aspect, almost a *raw material* (Saggio 2004).
The form, then, is only one dimension of interaction with the environment and, as such, is a state of transformation. In fact N.T., in thinking about architecture according to a *logical openness* to the concept of information (Licata 2008), ends by determining a progressive approach to the processes, organization, and rationalization of the living world. By describing the projects of N.T. through philosophical and, especially, psychoanalytic baggage, Roche seems to want to maintain a rigor and design technique behind his exciting narratives that is not only aimed at innovation but at continuous breakthroughs. N.T.'s architecture is, in fact, a constant conquest not so much of a new language as a mode of working with computers to crumble conventions, spoil contemporary myths, and, most importantly, to extend the field of interaction between the world and the human discipline of architecture itself. N.T., especially after the millennium, can boast a number of projects, some realized, others in the process of realization, and others which are still nuclei of research

in continual growth, contributions that advance the discipline like a silent and revolutionary heresy.

1.2 N.T.: Between the Surrealist Narrative and the Computer

In analyzing the dissemination and understanding of the information paradigm in architecture between the end of the nineties and the start of the new century, the emphasis on information has mainly concerned the computational power of the computer, almost exclusively understood as the capacity of generating and controlling form. In fact it is only with the birth and the brief but intense development of Cybernetics in the 1940's in the United States that the revolutionary idea of information as a common denominator between *soft and hard* science took shape.

For Norbert Wiener, who coined the term, *Cybernetics* was intended as a *science of the helm* (Wiener 1948) in the construction of models; thus, in the extraction and representation of information from reality, it is possible to recognize a new constructivist epistemology for dialogue with nature (Licata 2008).

In the architectural debate in the first decade of the new millennium, the emphasis is on the formal and productive potentials of the informatics instrument. Further, for the most astute critics, a new phase of research has been traced, an *interactive catalyst dimension* (Saggio 2007) resulting from the treatment and reciprocal transmission of information between spaces and users. The convergence of these common themes in the relationship between architecture and the world of the living, based on the crucial presence of information, is one of the most important results we can see in N.T.'s experience. Roche comes with a contemplation that already looks at nature, as is evident 15-16 in some of his projects which were elaborated in the nineties and which exhibit a clearly unsettled desire to root architecture in nature rather than to yield results based on forms of a certain complexity. These are projects that enhance the computer; indifferent by definition to energy and matter, they reveal the latent potential of the *instrument* to *converse* with nature.

These early projects of Roche, often overlooked by critics, are declarative in this sense. In the dialectic between architecture and nature, Roche includes the scope of constraint imposed by nature itself which, according to the best cybernetic tradition, can help with navigation once the constraints are assumed as *negative information* (Von Glasersfeld, 1994).

IN ANTAGONISM WITH NATURE

N.T. detects elements in nature which are suspicious, opposing, and malevolent. The architecture therefore, almost as if it were a new predator, is designed as a hidden or even secret construction equipped with the same antagonism of living species and the same mechanisms of defense and relative strategy.

GROWING UP, COMPIÈGNE, 1993
Elevation of the house and diagram of the growth of the trees (top to bottom).

CONTRACTIONS, LA PETITE FRANCE, 1996, REUNION ISLAND
Diagram of the deformation of the site (left). "Predatory effect" of the architecture in nature (top to bottom on the right).

FOLDING, SOWETO, SOUTH AFRICA, 1997
In this project the folding of the memorial-museum on the tomb of Hector Peterson is not a mere computation of an architectural form. Rather, it is a technique of recombining a geographic condition with a new random set of transparent elements, from which a new architectural place can emerge.

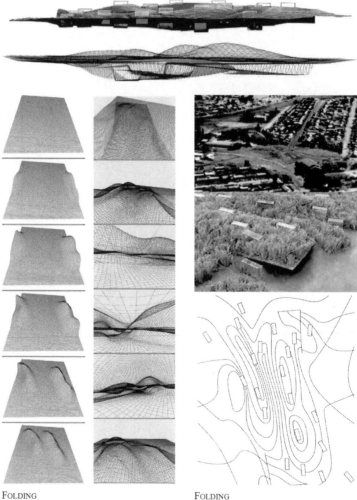

FOLDING

Profiles of the set (top); generative diagrams of the undulation of the soil (top to bottom).

FOLDING

Rendering of the reconstitution of the site (top) and plans of the complex (bottom).

Within this framework singular projects have been proposed, including architectures destined to die and dissolve into the forest or trees that silently invade and tear at the architectural shell (*Growing Up*, 1993). 15 These are images that emphasize a level of architecture which is radically different from that resulting from the echoes of the deconstructivist tradition. Already from these projects the distance is clear between N.T. and the other architectural firms that are beginning to work with ecological themes; the other offices recall a reassuring vision which is destined to result in a plethora of *green architecture* projects, or in those that base their form on the very use of algorithms inspired by biological processes of growth. For N.T., instead, the approach is that of seeing nature as suspect, to be uncovered through strategies that see the architecture almost as a new predator (*Contractions*, 1996), able to provide itself mechanisms of defense 15 and its own secretive strategies of antagonism such as those between living species. It is also the return of an approach in which the very elements of scientific discourse and *psycho-geographic* dimensions seek to coexist in a new methodological framework (*Folding*, 1997). 16 How can computational information be used in architecture to constitute a means for connecting the biological, perceptual, and psychological conditions? By contemplating the French Surrealist tradition and, in particular, psychoanalysis an incredible *protocol* is defined which is based on the mixture between information technologies and unconscious experience, and between metaphysics and biology, where the binding glue is the ability of the computer in the *transcription* of heterogeneous codes.

1.3 I've Heard About

In doing so, N.T. discovers its ability to mediate such dichotomic relations by introducing an apparatus that has a role in both the conceptual processes of the project as well as in those realized. Shrinking from the temptation to develop a new digital mannerism in architecture, N.T. identifies such an apparatus in the computational machine. This is not only considered productive in its Deleuzian sense as derived from Duchamp.

Although N.T. favors these references, the machine is also delegated to design and manage continuous transactions and to act as an intermediary between man and other systems, both living and artificial. Roche seems far from the categories which, in the last fifteen years, have attempted to harness architectural experimentation in a new

methodology of form, based in a renewed interest in the parametric
approach which here may also constitute a component part of the
project. Even in the first few projects in which there is a stated purpose
for the computer (*Overflow,* at the end of the nineties or, again,
16 *Folding* in 1997) we do not find the rhetoric of a new hyper-connected
world. Rather, computational ability is engaged to reconfigure
geomorphologic support, also seen as the possibility to create a new
geography that can adhere to the logics of the program in use. It is a
slow process that even in smaller projects shows that, for N.T., the
digitalization of information means to understand the logic of
interaction of phenomena, more than the form they eventually assume.
The machine, then, is not only an mechanical apparatus delegated to
transforming labor into energy, but above all a new artifact able to
process, produce, and exchange information. In its constitutive
platform of exchange, it can interrogate the scientific dimension of
nature and lead it to the realm of architecture; their code shares
computational information. This is the intuition that was formed after
the first design experiences and which distanced the group from more
consolidated research. In order to understand how this framework is
formed we must abandon a chronological discourse and investigate
20 one of the most well-known and discussed projects of N.T., *I've heard
about.* It is among the most interesting speculations and research of this
period, almost an epistemological and methodological conquest by the
group.

To some extent inspired by Constant's program *New Babylon,* the
project *I've heard about* won the competition FEIDAD 2005-6, at the
right time and with its own international research platform in
architecture that was designed in the paradigm of information. Roche
understands immediately that if the presence of a network affects
the architecture this relation, in addition to its sociological or
methodological logic, is a cognitive problem, which concerns the
transcription of the network's *rhizomatic space* into the physical, into
the architectural and urban. If we think that the network, as a model,
describes the multiple interactions between humans and between
humans and machines, we can also understand the power and
fascination in it being raised as a paradigm for architecture. If the
computer is an excellent tool to represent models of complexity (one
thinks of the simulations of swarms) it is likewise true that its intrinsic
capacity to form networks makes it by definition also a means of
production of complexity. *I've heard about,* then, foremost emphasizes

the exchange, transaction, and, especially, the possibility that information is otherwise incorporated (*embodied*) and exchanged in physical objects according to a city project based on a model of the network of connection between machines, human beings, architecture, and the continuous interactions that occur. This proposal for settlement is the visionary city that N.T. sees as a response to the discussion between the presence of the network and the possible physical repercussions in the formation of the city. If several authors have described a new world made of flows and fluxes, painting a *liquidity* of the city that is more abstract than material, Roche addresses the problem inversely, questioning how the multiple interactions that take place in information exchange platforms may be materially constitutive for a settlement. Thus it stands as the first condition that the settlement is generated through *bottom-up* logic, inscribed in a sort of social and territorial contract between inhabitants and an architectural structure (also called *bio-structure*) that hosts them.

In *I've heard about* the *protocol*, a term that Roche uses to describe the behaviors and relationships on which the projects were founded, is social and, even more precisely, *bio-political* (Roche 2005). We also emphasize that the word *protocol* is to be understood in its technical sense as well as political, as these are the protocols that allow different devices and entities to communicate with each other.

The central idea is that the residents of I've *heard about* produce crucial information in various transactions that would consequently affect the logical formation of the architecture. How to materialize a reasoning of this kind? As the first group to have the brilliant idea of pairing a robot with architecture, N.T. invented the VIAB, a [20] constructor agent which implements these logics in correspondence with the complex negotiations that take place between the people and the city itself, mediated by the machine.

The vast social protocol underlying the negotiations, to which turn for a more detailed reading, is nothing more than the writing of a series of rules between people and machines, which are continually validated through the exchange of information. Thus, human beings, robots, and material produced through their concerted architecture itself, which is constantly changing, continual transformation, are a result of continual renegotiation.

The city might rise or fall, or even be destroyed, since the arborescent [22] organization on which it is based, is produced automatically by the

I'VE HEARD ABOUT, 2005

A settlement as a process resulting from bottom-up logic, implemented by humans, robots, and materials, mediated in their negotiations by the machine which is able to process any different and contradictory information that has been put into play.

I'VE HEARD ABOUT

A picture of the possible development of the settlement after some time (top). Prototypes of the structure in stereolithography (bottom left), and the robot VIAB in action along the structure in five frames (bottom right).

robot VIAB on the basis of requests from the citizens. To introduce a
robot as a builder and negotiator has huge significance. It means, first
of all, to *incorporate* the computer into a physical agent whose aim is
transformative, which implies its ability to physically produce
architecture in real time with the same fluidity to which the network
and information processing have accustomed us. Finally, it is the
possibility to translate the outcome of the transactions into certain
transformations, through a final synthesis produced by the decisions of
VIAB according to an algorithm. How this synthesis comes about is the
result of a delicate and significant issue that is interwoven within the
history of Information Technology, robotics, programming, and
Artificial Intelligence. The centrality of the operation is, in fact, in
VIAB's capacity to act as intermediary between the people and the [20]
environment since this robot performs, during its operations, a
continuous reevaluation of local conditions, from the weather to the
density attained by structure, and can also use materials available
locally to perform the transformations. These capabilities are provided
by the algorithm that governs the robot, which is defined in a long *script*
(available on N.T.'s web-site), which is one of the most fascinating
aspects of the operation.

The *script*, in fact, not only serves to generate form, but also to describe
possible interactions on the occurrence of behaviors; in this way, on the
basis of requests from the citizens immersed in the structure through
an interface, the VIAB is directed to the manufacturing of new nuclei.
The algorithm, among other things, is also *open source*, which means
that under suitable conditions the inhabitants can change its nature or
even reset it.

The VIAB, far from being pure science-fiction speculation, bases the
success of its operations on an experimental construction technique
called *contour crafting*, developed at the *University of Southern* [22]
California, which has aroused considerable interest: the robot, in fact,
through a nozzle injection, is able to trace the contours of a shape and
then to secrete a liquid material. The contours thus operate as
formwork for the subsequent layers through a construction which
proceeds by horizontal sections. The system also allows
reprogramming during the phases of construction, theoretically
providing for the manufacture of very tall buildings.

Inspired by a phasmid (*phasmatodea*), the well-known insect capable
of camouflaging itself, the VIAB is a *situated* robot, which means that it
bases its actions on the *features* available in the environment. It moves [20-22]

I'VE HEARD ABOUT, 2005

The complex looks like a layered structure, rich with concavities, an organic form that resembles coral reefs. There is no hierarchical and representative structure. The voids will be completed by residential kits able to ensure even the conduct of agricultural activities.

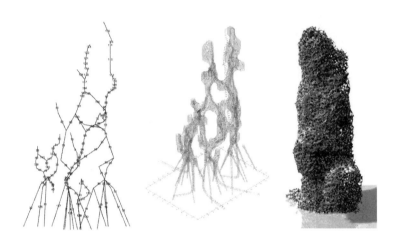

I'VE HEARD ABOUT

Later stages of the model derived by the algorithm: from the branching to the casing (top). Project drawings of the various parts of VIAB (bottom). The robot, a key part of the project, does not constitute a merely speculative part but instead is carefully designed with the collaboration of experts in robotics.

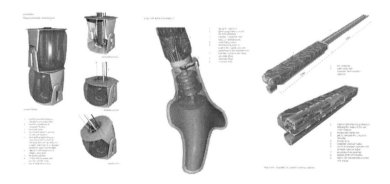

along the structure along tracks (similar to those of a crane) that enable it, iteratively and on the basis of transactions in progress, to continually transform the structure through additive or subtractive processes (the protocol requires that every ten years the parts are destroyed, and, if necessary, restarted).

Although this community (the robots, the citizens, and the produced structure) through a system of relations that unites them, could be understood according to its organizational model of complexity like that of *swarm intelligence*, the dimensions raised by this project are in actuality even more sophisticated, delineating the city as a phenomenon *emerging* from the interactions between machines and people, and not from decision-making processes based on the presence of an authority.

1.4 Determinism and Indeterminism, Strategies of Uncertainty

The resulting complex is presented as a stratified structure, an organic form that resembles the coral reefs and in which it is difficult to identify a hierarchy. The structure, full of voids and connective spaces, is completed with residential kits that consist of light-weight shell made from polymers. The kits are also equipped to handle the performance of agricultural activities. It is an architecture that is far from any intelligible pattern, or from any representative will: the subsystems that form it cannot be singled-out without losing the value of unity. But how is it that a system that relies on an algorithm and robots for its realization can produce a structure that is so organic and adheres to the logic of nature? Ignazio Licata, Italian physicist, points out that the limits of the cognitive systems that work in an algorithmic manner processing information from the symbolic and computational perspective are in the *logical-informational* closure of these systems (Licata 2008).

The computer, and in general the algorithmic procedures, are not able to produce new codes or to expand their semantic domains during operation. The information, in other words, is always the same and is based on the same code. In contrast, a cognitive and biologic system processes information not in a computational way, but shows different and continuous openings in the environment, taking into account the history of the interactions it has had with it. The system in this case proceeds to a continuous *encoding* and *decoding* of information, resulting in the expansion of its semantic domain, and creating new codes (Licata 2008).

To understand the VIAB as a pure executor of a project conceived up top would be to fall into a logic by which the resulting architecture would consist in a task brutally executed by the machine.

How to overturn this principle? Roche understands that the strength and the weakness of scientific models simulated by the computer is in the absence of noise, and in the ideal conditions that reproduce. In other words, their weakness is in their determinism. In a real city, however, it is the immense noise of information that produces constant complexity. He also introduces, as disruptive elements and real sources of uncertainty, two fundamental ingredients: the first is the stochastic nature of the algorithm that models the behavior of VIAB; the second, to be considered central, is the human presence of the inhabitants, considered not only as mere bearers of a need. Sources of noise or of other information are thus introduced, and affect the constructive process of the architecture.

In place of the industrial robot, a productive machine in chains, another robot is substituted that operates in a probabilistic manner able to take into account the noise of reality, and to direct the continuous change of direction away from any determinism. What type of information is it that the inhabitants convey? The citizens of the structure, defined as the *vectors and protectors of this complexity* (Roche 2005), in addition to communicating with VIAB through an interface of input data, are in fact literally intercepted by the structure. Here Roche introduces a theme that reveals how the relationship between information and biology can be explored in architecture. Based on the concept of *biofeedback*, which concerns the adaptation of the organism in order to maintain a state of dynamic equilibrium with its environment, nano-receptors are dispersed within the structure. Once inhaled, according the stress present in the organism, particular molecules are released from it. These, identified by a spectroscope which measures their density, provide information about the level of stress of the inhabitants that then disrupt the behavior of the robot. The VIAB, thus, the acronym of which does not by chance mean *viability* and *variability*, is continually forced to redefine its own strategies, adapting to environmental, electrical, and chemical inputs, even contradictory ones, from which it produces by synthesis the specific steps to be taken in the construction of the structure and in the reasonableness of its actions.

1.5 The Mind of the Living vs. The Artificial Mind

In effect *I've heard about* anticipates and creatively addresses crucial issues related to Information Technology in architecture, and first of all those resulting from the *computationalist* cultural setting which is the one that has absorbed the mind and, therefore, the cognitive processes of the computer, and from which the paradigm of Artificial Intelligence derives. Matters that would seemingly not affect architects are rather crucial when we describe design methods in architecture that place at the center of their actions the presence of Information and its processing. The cognitive sciences, from their birth in the seventies to their later branching, appear divided between the proposal of a model of the mind similar to a computer, and one closer to biology which considers the mind deeply rooted in the body and even extended into the context (*embodied*). This schematic division is actually the synthesis of a more complex constellation of scientific positions on different sides, that contribute to defining the theoretical and conceptual background for the technological implementation of concepts such as those of intelligence, reasoning, interaction, and life. Disciplines such robotics, automation, and interface design owe much to the Cognitive Science, which form the theoretical and philosophical soul of the Information Technology Revolution. Roche seems to capture the apparent contradiction between a protocol that is founded on a deterministic computational model (that of the growth of the structure), and the immense noise of interactions and human desires. He admits to the principle that the computer tool draws its strength from its coupling with the human agent, realizing that the computer is basically a very accurate model of the mind but profoundly limited; the investigation and disruption of these limits is crucial. If in *I've heard about*, in fact, the emphasis is placed on the exchange of information between the bodies of the inhabitants and the evolution of the structure, it is interesting to know by what mind these bodies are equipped. How to interact with the components furthest from computational logic but closer to those that are actually human?

If the structure is based on an algorithmic protocol, although *open source* and *indeterministic*, within which protocol does the mind of the inhabitants occur? Coming from a culture that is more continental than American, for Roche the inhabitants are not only defined as *users* referring to the strictly scientific cognitive logic in the Galilean sense, but are minds in the most inclusive sense, the psychoanalytic. Even special psychic states of the citizens, from sleepwalking to hypnosis, are

HYPNOTIC CHAMBER, MAM, PARIS 2005

A constituent component of I've heard about is achieved through the manufacturing of pieces using a 5-axis machine. The room obtained is used for a hypnotic session, part of the same experimental protocol.

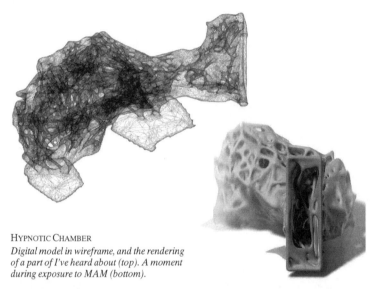

HYPNOTIC CHAMBER
Digital model in wireframe, and the rendering of a part of I've heard about (top). A moment during exposure to MAM (bottom).

thus introduced into the project as further cognitive activity to be taken into account. Roche believes them to be, on the one hand, necessary conditions to feel part of the whole and, on the other, to confuse the machine through information related to non-rational dimensions, which are dreamlike and expanded with respect to the cognitive domain of the machine itself.

This breach in protocol, apparently certain of the scientific validity of computationalism, thus comes to be exalted in the realization of the prototype of *Hypnochamber*, an installation realized at the Museum of ²⁶ Modern Art in Paris in 2005, which, in addition to materializing an architectural piece that is constitutive of *I've heard about*, aims to instill in visitors a state of *social dis-alienation*. Through prototyping techniques for the manufacture of components for parts and their assembly, the installation is mounted to form an enveloping structure in which visitors can perform a *hypnotic* session, which in the complete project should provide VIAB with additional information. The machine is once again contradicted by the exchange of less-objective and more-conceivably subjective information. It is important to note, however, that the *Hypnochamber* is dialectically opposed to *I've heard about,* constituting the countercheck to the latter's feasibility.

If the first seems an urban experiment born in the utopian tradition of architecture, the hypnosis room, which for Roche is a *heterotopia,* already shows in a very clear manner that the *logical openness* of the different systems in play in the project corresponds to a production of complexity, and thus to new possibilities. The agent, living in the scene both as a designer and user, is what disrupts the protocol itself, which helps to expands its semantic domains and brings a new code to the system, possibly in a capillary manner. There is no language, then, but information.

2. Embedding Information in a Context

2.1 Embodiment and Hyper-Localism
The eruption onto the contemporary architectural scene of a proposal like *I've heard about,* founded on a full negotiation between information procedures for listening to the inhabitants and of responses from the architecture in terms of transformation, highlights the *constructivist* nature of information as a common basis on which to build relationships. The constructivist approach, in fact, considers impossible the existence of objective truths outside of a theoretical frame of reference and without the presence of subjects able to attribute meanings. If *I've heard about* can be considered a manifesto of N.T. and the setting of research of the group, it should be noted how this belies a series of positions related to Information Technology and to the use of the computer in architecture. These positions have emphasized the acritical ease with which the computer is used in design processes. Some authors in particular have denounced the presence of the computer as essentially an accessory underlining the gap between the tactile sensibility of the body and the abstraction of the computer instrument (Pallasmaa 2005).

These considerations, which have had the merit of raising the issue of Information Technology in architecture in a critical manner, seem, however, to rest upon a conception of the instrument that is perhaps poorly understood with respect to the huge developments that, in recent decades, have regarded the computer from a theoretical-philosophical point of view.

Even more critical approaches within the cognitive sciences, linked closely to the development of Computer Science, have placed in the center of their own reflection the limits of a computationalist setting of cognition. They propose new contributions, such as the idea of the mind as a network, by basing this *connectionism* on the biological model of neural networks, and above all in robotics - the *embodied* - where the mind and thus cognition are never separated from the fact of residing in a body (and not in a computer), or of being situated in an *environment*.

Consequently the development of related technologies, above all robotics, have evolved in these directions, proposing systems that are increasingly capable of communicating with their environment, and which increasingly configure themselves as ecological networks of relations that do not function like electronic machines separate from the context. In particular, this *embodied* approach is founded on the crucial fact of possessing a body situated in an environment that is by definition ecologic. This approach does not place, at the center of cognitive experience, a simulation of the environment which is detached on the part of the organism or the artificial agent, but rather the organism itself and its *psychological, historical, and sensorimotor experience* within that environment. (Varela, Thompson and Rosch, 1991). The information then appears no longer as an elaboration of data by an external agent that represents and processes it, as much as the set of relationships that an agent endowed with a body has with the environment of which it is a part.

The value of these positions is clear in the rest of the approach based on the concepts of system, environment, and the exchange of information found in different branches of ecological thought as early as the seventies. It is also found in the idea of knowledge as the result of a reciprocal interaction between observer and observed such as in *Constructivism*, but with different consequences in architecture. Yet it is in the design experience of N.T. that these concepts inaugurate a convincing approach.

If the information in architecture allows for the establishment of links between different components and among different transformative moments, these links inevitably concern nature. These are the ways in which architecture is rooted in a context or, on the contrary, imposes itself onto it, triggering controllable relations on a new level and made possible by a technology that can manipulate the different dimensions of information present. One emblematic case is the *Green Gorgon* project created for the competition for the New Museum of the Beaux-Arts in Lausanne, Switzerland (2005), where N.T., aware that it is 30 working with the presence of different systems, seems to appeal to many possible relationships, including the dreamlike. This project is initially explained by the authors by resorting to the body of phasmids with regard to distribution and general articulation, then to Ophelia's body made famous by one of the most beautiful poems of Rimbaud and by Millais's painting.

The museum is planned for a site on Lake Geneva where, as the architects emphasize, it is not easy to distinguish between the natural and anthropogenic landscape; the area has already been torn in part by waters, and there have been several transformations.

For N.T., attentive to the subtle but significant differences between anthropological-cultural and scientific categories, the area should not

GREEN GORGON, LAUSANNE, 2005

Through a computational procedure not only is biology enabled but the project is placed in the broader context which is relevant to biodynamics. In place of a traditional reading of the landscape a more scientific one is preferred, which allows for connecting the vegetation of the project with that already existing, based on the natural-anthropogenic relationship.

GREEN GORGON
Accommodation of the building on the banks of the lake (top). Three-dimensional model of the new plant vegetation (on the side).

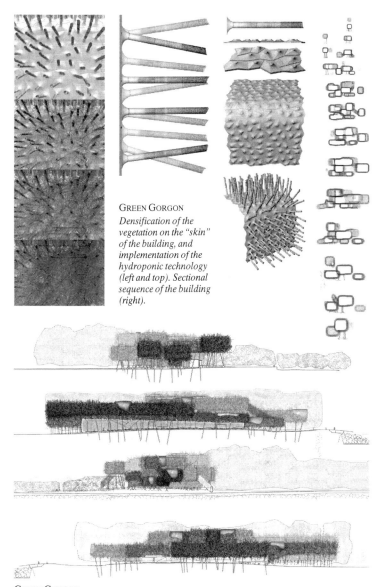

GREEN GORGON
*Densification of the
vegetation on the "skin"
of the building, and
implementation of the
hydroponic technology
(left and top). Sectional
sequence of the building
(right).*

GREEN GORGON
Four facades by which the building is articulated in the area.

be analyzed in terms of the landscape but in ecological terms, thus
coming to be identified as a *biotope lake* (Roche 2005). Information is
then extracted using a scientific as well as cultural reading.

The project, thus, contrary to the architecture language of recent
contemporary museums, seeks to make the building itself become
another living species, or to constitute one of the members of a
community that help to define the local ecosystem. Rather than acting
as a new element in the landscape, the architecture becomes a system
30-31 capable of continuing the specific *biocenosis*. The plant associations
that are located along the shores of the lake are articulated by N.T.
according to a double logic aimed at highlighting, on the one hand, the
categories that describe the possible relationships between man and
nature and, on the other, their willingness to give life to a system.
Within this articulation, the museum is composed according to a logic
of free disposition between parallelepipeds, both in plan and in section,
supporting different directions that form a network extended along the
longitudinal axes of the volumes that host various functions. A
labyrinthine architecture is obtained, a large-scale capillary system,
which denies any possible *panoptic* organization. Computer
technology, seemingly distant from a project that would seem romantic
in its dense literary allusions, plays, however, a fundamental role in the
construction of biocenosis and in the maintenance of the biotope.

How to transform architecture into one of the members of a
community that define a context? In the *Green Gorgon* museum N.T.,
perhaps the first to complete an operation of this type, identified in the
skin of the architectural organism the most suitable place to give life to
a coexistence between plant species and artificial elements. Through
31 *Voronoi tessellation*, an algorithmic process that serves to subdivide a
geometric region, a dense division of the entire external surface of the
museum is obtained. At the center of every micro-region extend
micro-drilled pipettes, devices capable of enabling the growth of plants
through a hydroponics system which cover the entire building. The
photosynthetic processes consequently help to purify and recycle
wastewater. The processing of information is thus transferred into the
preparation of a platform surface which is capable of transforming the
entire building within the environment that it intended to modify. In
the architecture it recognizes a possible biological identity and enables
it to co-participate in the natural cycles of the place. Through a
computer procedure, not only biology is enabled but the project is
resolved in the broader context and relevance of of biodynamics.

Some elements made of EFTE pierce the surface, allowing light to enter and raising bubbles in the green skin.

Users of the museum are consequently regarded as living agents constituting part of the same community. Visitors losing themselves in the labyrinthine space are equipped with a device that acts both as a navigation system and as a carrier of information pertaining to the exhibit. Navigating in the museum offers an experience that shows how important it is to get lost in order to acquire new knowledge, being able, however, to continually readjust the course. The building is, therefore, also a metaphor of cybernetics. The computer techniques, rather than being seen as facilitators for formal creation, become the tool capable of creating the boundary conditions to make the building penetrate into its context and incorporate itself radically in it.

2.2 Protocols of Disappearance

If the rootedness of a building in its context is also a traditional experience of architecture, a *hyper-localism* like that realized in *Green Gorgon* seems to actually determine a *disappearance* of the building in its context. This is not *mimesis* or a romantic loss in the landscape, but quite a different way of working with the information available. As we shall see in other projects it is also the recreation of the context made possible by the availability of different information and the ability of the architect to know how to place it in radical relation through computer techniques. In fact, in N.T.'s projects the disappearance of the building in its environment is always for pragmatic reasons. One example is the project *Shearing*, made in Sommières in France in 2003, [34] where such tension was born from the need to comply with the laws in force regarding the conservation of the landscape, while still not renouncing the realization of architecture. The house is thus covered in a green casing of materials used for agriculture, which returns information relating to the morphology of support. This casing shows the flexibility of the computer's calculation not in reconstituting a new form, but in the continuity of the geomorphological support that the architecture had claimed to interrupt.

It is, however, in the project *Spidernethewood*, created in Nîmes in [35] 2007, that disappearance as a technique is accomplished in a more radical manner, by continuing certain premises outlined in *Green Gorgon*. The project involves a two-story house, 400sqm with a swimming pool, immersed in the French countryside. A parallelepiped body, the residence is divided and crossed by a cruciform gallery that

SHEARING SOMMIÈRES, 2003, FRANCE

The house is lined with a green casing as those commonly used in agriculture, which returns information relating to the morphology of the support.

SHEARING

Views of the casing in the landscape, and a view of the interior (top to bottom on the left, and top). Generative studies, the material used in the casing and elevations (below).

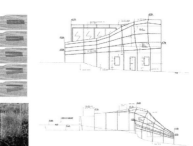

SPIDERNETHEWOOD NÎMES, FRANCE 2007
A known procedure of computational design, meshing, is used in this project to accommodate nature and to densify it. The vegetation will cover the architecture completely over time.

SPIDERNETHEWOOD
Ground plan of the house immersed in nature, and a model of the covering and of the gallery (top). Views of the complex from the outside and inside, after 5 years (right and bottom).

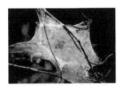

makes the external penetrate into the internal, producing a typological continuity reminiscent of some contemporary research on complex surfaces.

35 This gallery continues outside, tracing the corridors on the borders of the lot, opening to the sky for several spans, and in correspondence with the pool. Innervated into the inert block of the house as well, the gallery is designed through a *mesh* system that, bending and densifying the polygons, is able to shrink and expand. The purpose of this connective space is simultaneously as a support and boundary for the rich vegetation that grows around the house. A known computational design technique, *meshing*, is then used in an effective manner to accommodate nature and, in fact, to help it grow. The gallery is made with a metal structure to which cling polygons made of polypropylene. The apparent paradox here between the cold computational techniques and the heat of the living systems, so typical in N.T.'s work, is further visible in its intervention plan: in the gallery a reversal is achieved in favor of nature. It is the house, in fact, that becomes *empty* while the vegetation, undisturbed over the years, will be free to follow its own life cycles of destruction and regeneration. In this complex system, therefore, the history of the system itself becomes central. Perhaps it is for this reason that Roche asked the celebrated science-fiction writer Bruce Sterling to write a piece on the house, set in the future year 2030.

If this project embodies the idea of the return of a biotope that is
37 already anticipated in *Green Gordon*, the project *I'mlostinParis,* for the construction of a house in an urban setting in the heart of Paris in 2009, is even more radical in realizing these concepts in an architecture. What happens if the camouflage hut used by *duck hunters* is placed in an urban environment? If the image of a hut is a counterproposal to the *duck* of Venturian memory for which form follows meaning, for N.T. the problem of the covering and appearance of the architecture is the opposite; not only does the meaning not correspond in any way with the shape, but it is part of a more delicate problem, deep-rooted in the ecological, social, and cultural antagonism of that extraordinary phenomenon that we call a city. The property is built according to a section of three floors, of which one is underground and grows on a rectangle leaning against a wall structure, which leaves an L-shaped empty space. On the ground floor the living area with kitchen, living room, and services are distributed longitudinally and on the upper floors are the sleeping areas.

I'MLOSTINPARIS, 2009, PARIS

This project is designed on the mobilization of processes from the unpredictable outcomes between the natural and artificial. A biological process is created at the microscopic scale; along with this, there is that between the plants and inhabitants of the house, up to the one between the house and city, at a macroscopic scale. These couplings are still undetermined since, in such relationships between species, one of them may succumb at any moment.

I'MLOSTINPARIS

Images of the containers that, in addition to collecting rain water and feeding the plants, also cause a pleasant diffused light inside the rooms. Each container is made of blown glass (top). The house in the urban Parisian environment (bottom).

The two floors are connected by a staircase which follows the same longitudinal logic, shouldering the wall. The result is a prismatic body, approximately 4.5x14 meters. This, however, constitutes only the inert core of a more complex organization, which is solved by a subsequent casing intended to house a collection of living systems in the antagonism between them and the city. A network is anchored to the
37 walls on a metallic frame. The development of this surface results in an apparatus on which a colony of living materials is established, including 1,200 ferns and 300 blown-glass containers that allow for hydroponic cultivation using rainwater.

Another invisible colony is housed inside another 200 containers. In this case it is a special bacteria (*Rhizobium*) which, through certain processes of symbiosis, fixes nitrogen in the plants and promotes their growth, thereby avoiding chemical solutions for as long as possible. In this way a biological process of microscopic size is mobilized, together with that between the plants and the residents of the house on the human scale, up to the last between the house and the city at a macroscopic scale. This couplings are still undetermined, however, as they are able to degenerate at any moment and reach a point at which one of the species succumbs. The information put into play by this system, therefore, concerns different scales of observation; moving from antagonism to symbiosis in a continuous dynamic equilibrium, architecture as the silhouette of an object in a space ceases to exist. On the one hand the house as an urban phenomenon dissolves, not even having a facade anymore, and on the other hand it manifests as a mass of living material, suspicious and unexpected between the silhouettes of the other buildings in Paris.

2.3 ....Or of Apparition?

Roche seems to suggest that information remains indeterminate until an observer attributes it significance. Thus the project *I'mlostinParis*, playing on the edge of the disappearance of the building, would paradoxically also result in its own unexpected appearance within the city. Other design experiences of N.T. tend to emphasize, in this regard, perceptual and cognitive dimension, relying on latent information in any site and at any scale. So a 2003 project for a holiday home, by a couple of art collectors on the island of Trinidad in the
40 Caribbean (*Mosquito Bottleneck*), rather than being characterized as a type of architecture of holiday homes, is rooted in the tropical environment of the island in a creative manner. It is a place

characterized by nature that is less reassuring and gentle than that of temperate regions. The presence of a local threat, that of the mosquito carrying the Western Nile virus, appears to result in a further *logical openness* of the concept of interaction with the site which, this time, converges on a carrier in the animal kingdom. An analysis of the environment previously conducted through reassuring ecological categories is here poisoned by suspicion and paranoia, given the presence of the infectious carrier. Rather than giving rise to a defensive attitude, however, insight into this invisible danger can lead to a new coexistence of different levels of design.

Introducing a psychic element into the reading of the information available, one realizes how *uncanny* the presence of the insect is, and ends by negotiating with it. N.T., therefore, assumes the more dangerous interaction between the new residents and the environment to be fundamental. Inspired by a custom prevalent among the inhabitants of the region, which consists in cutting a bottle into two 40 parts to insert the upper half into the lower by inverting it, N.T. conceives of a housing device that is both a protective conduit for the residents of the new house and a deadly trap for mosquitos. The information needed for the physical generation of this tube, that of assimilating into the model, ends coherently by regarding the probabilistic trajectories of this local dangerous carrier. The tiny insect moves in a space according to trajectories which are unpredictable for humans, but palpable as an enveloping danger in the sense of bodily perception. The information that N.T. extracts, then, is in fact related to danger posed to the body, as if to say that this is essential for its survival.

The trajectories of danger are then transcribed into the tube through a network of splines, and from this a double enveloping surface is made which designates the safe space of the house. Using the simple polyethylene tube described creates, on the one hand, internal spaces for the life of the owners and, on the other, creates traps for mosquitos in the concavity open to the outside by following in principle the same device created by the locals. It is funnel-shaped opening which the unfortunate mosquitos can travel in only one direction: the one which will to their death.

The polyethylene produces a space of safety and comfort and, through its transparency, allows the inner space to participate in the lush environment of nature outside, although also revealing the trap mechanism. It thus appears an *ecological* device for negotiation

MOSQUITO BOTTLENECK, TRINIDAD, 2003

The information that N.T. extracts from the site is, in fact, related to the danger to the human body, meaning that it is essential to its survival. The trajectories of danger are then transcribed into the tube through a network of splines, and from this a double enveloping surface is made which creates two spaces: a safe space in the house for humans, and a deadly one for mosquitos.

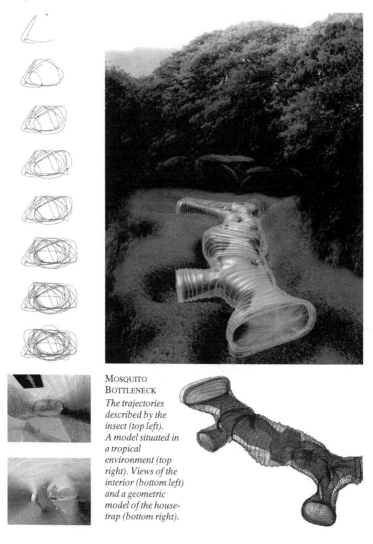

MOSQUITO BOTTLENECK

The trajectories described by the insect (top left). A model situated in a tropical environment (top right). Views of the interior (bottom left) and a geometric model of the house-trap (bottom right).

HE SHOT ME DOWN, KOREA, 2006-2007
*A rendering of the complex, a wire-frame model of the building, and transporter robots of
biomass (top). Integration of the building into the hill (center). Model of the project
emphasizing the ballistic effect (bottom).*

between the death of the mosquitos and the death avoided by the inhabitants. Although this function has been described by Roche and some critics (Corbellini 2009) as a *sadomasochistic* negotiation, in our view what matters is the relationship with nature, which is revealed in the less-reassuring aspects of submission and domination between species, as well as what can be managed extracting otherwise-irrelevant information in the more conventional processes of the reading of the context. N.T. therefore continually contemplates diseases and errors to reiterate that perception and cognition are to be considered two dimensions of the same concept of information.

[41] The project *He shot me down* in 2007 is based on this reasoning. The program concerns the construction of a small functional mixed unit consisting in a residence, a small museum, a restaurant, a shop, and a dance center, to be built near the demilitarized region on the border between the two Koreas in Heyri.

The information assumed concerns ballistic effect, taken from physics that studies the movement of projectiles. This is an unhappy memory for the site, but here it borrows from the volume of the mountain and generates a topological surface characterized by a series of orifices that seem to represent the speed of the projectile, its inertia, and its destructive fury.

At the same time it also generates openings for light and access. A robot coupled with the structure runs along the dangerous bordering area, gathering biomass that is then deposited onto the building, thus helping to improve the insulation.

The transcription of information regarding danger, both in terms of ballistics and in the ability to traverse minefields using the robot, even produces, according to the author, a certain eroticization of the project (the projectile that penetrates the mountain), that results from the attribution of a value to a situation which would not apparently have it. In this way N.T. reaffirms the psychic value of the experience, the polysemy of meanings of the project and architectural design, and the multiplicity of dimensions that architecture is able to offer to the human experience.

A similar methodology that introduces computational information to the richness of the psyche can be found in other projects. In [43] *Thegardenofearthlydelights*, a project for Lopud in Croatia in 2008, the garden behind the monastery is conceptualized as a combination of a computational procedure that simulates a lava flow, and of the arrangement of plants in relation to their degrees of toxicity.

THE GARDEN OF EARTHLY DELIGHTS, LOPUD, CROATIA, 2008
Three-dimensional section of the garden and details of the area dedicated to the alchemical machines.

BROOMWITCH, MEUDON, FRANCE 2008
Design of the garden with the extension of the house that is being proposed as a new growth to be accessed by a path (left column). The robot mimetic conveyor in three configurations that it assumes according to the geomorphological variations of the support (right column).

The lava flow produces a space, to be built in pillows made of EFTE, consistent with the geomorphologic support; different plants located inside are then paired with certain machines that would make it possible to distill spirits. This would cause, however, a reaction of *suspicion* in the visitors; the reactivation of a historical site and its conservation become possible only as long as they exacerbate and 43 manipulate information related to hazard. In *Broomwitch* in 2008, an extension of a house of André Bloc now on the property occupied by the Seroussi family, a vortex is being developed which is equipped with hydroponic tentacles and which is empty at the center, able to accommodate a museum. A strange vehicle capable of transforming itself through a camouflage procedure tuned to the environment would transport visitors from Bloc's house to the new *monstrous growth* (Roche 2008).

The information in these projects becomes a shimmering reflection in the game of mirrors between the project, the designer, and the client, which transcends the neutral computational processing of data and is continuously open to the possible implications of meanings of design in architecture.

This psychoanalytical game interrupts the semantic richness of living systems within the abstract logic of computation. It also seems to emphasize the indeterminate nature of information, and its susceptibility to appear and disappear in relation to the cognitive domain of the observers (designers or users).

2. 4 The Fine Dust of Information - Order and Disorder

If information in Shannon's classical theory (Shannon 1948) is associated with the order or, negatively, with the disorder (entropy) of a system, and if for certain authors information can be defined as the *raw material of architecture* (Saggio 2004), we can understand another of N.T.'s projects. It is aimed at the introduction of greater order in an environment with high entropy, which is a reality typical of emergent contemporary megalopolises.

46 *Dustyrelief* is the project of a museum of contemporary art in Bangkok, Thailand, developed in 2002, which relies once again on one of the most negative aspects of the city: its high degree of pollution. Even before the program the atmosphere of the city is assessed, and found to be so full of dust and CO_2 that its electromagnetic spectrum seems to be limited only to the scale of grays.

The negative presence of these particle elements suspended in the air unleashes the project idea. The museum (around 5,000 msq of useable area) is dealt with according to a strategic plan that aims for a functional mix able to use environments in a flexible and independent way. Simple bodies are organized on a tripartite area, and run parallel 46 to the long side, with the central portion elevated higher.

There is a connective system made of ramps and staircases which run toward and alongside the central body, and through it in diagonal directions. Various functions are thus distributed linearly, from the exhibition halls to the auditorium, to the rooms for administration and services. A system of smaller volumes, variously inclined and strategically extruding upwards, pierce the parallelepipeds creating shafts of light.

This is a neutral space, designed avoiding a characterization that could interfere with future expositions. It results in a design which is far from the emphasis of the architectural language of the author as carried out by many *archistars* during the last few years. Nonetheless, the aggregation of Euclidean volumes is covered by a mesh that creates a casing of its topology, full of concavities between the edges of the parallelepipeds.

This is actually a network of aluminum equipped with an electrostatic system; once activated, this system is able to exploit the noted effect, and to capture dust suspended in the atmosphere. The building thus manifests its presence acting as a giant magnet that can attract a dense *cultivation of dust particles*, which are able, once accumulated on the mesh, to condition the interior of the building and to act as a filter of the gradation of light.

The reading of information regarding the nature of these particulates as a potential already in place allows the establishment of a meaningful relationship with the environment. From the entropy of a mixture in suspension (state of disorder), the building acts as the ordering agent in this context. By charging itself with energy and capturing dust, it constructs a new level of information in the urban environment. This is certainly an image of the complexity that Roche proposed in this project, since it is the huge number of components in play that make the form emerge by the laws of attraction. Perhaps it is the first image of this kind to appear in architecture, apart from Diller and Scofidio's *Blur* for the Swiss Expo in the same year, whose complex form appears to be motivated by aesthetic reasons rather than substantial ones, as in the case of N.T..

ARCHITECTURAL
PROTOTYPES OF THE
COMPLEXITY
PARADIGM
DUSTYRELIEF/B_MU,
BANGKOK, THAILAND,
2002

The reading of information as a potential already in place allows for the establishment of a meaningful relationship with the environment. From the entropy of a mixture in suspension (state of disorder), the building acts as an ordering agent charging itself from energy and building a new level of information that appears in the urban environment. It is certainly an image of complexity.

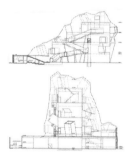

DUSTYRELIEF/B_MU
The image offered from the building covered with dust (top). Urban elevation, conceptual section and a prototype of the electrostatic network (center). Sections and plans (bottom).

2.5 Disappear - Appear - Detach

A design thinking able to create an architecture from the dust dispersed in the urban atmosphere certainly owes very much to an articulated research in which Roche and N.T. seem to retain information in a new *language of science* (Von Baeyer 2005), using the correlation between energy and matter in architecture. Outcomes which now seem almost obvious had already been addressed by N.T. as far back as 2001. One thinks of the famous *(Un)plug*, a building [48] prototype commissioned by the *Électricité de France (EDF)*, with the aim of developing architectural solutions for the supply of energy from renewable sources.

The program is relatively simple. It is, in fact, an office building. Roche understands that he must make use of a logical system, considering the outermost covering of the building as a place for exchange between energy and information. Thus he adopts the metaphor of the skin, subjecting it to a radical view and imagining it as *overexposed, burned by the sun and mottled by cancerous and degenerative mutations* (Roche 2001).

This metaphor, which introduces a pathological state, actually serves to define two stratagems that optimize the procurement of energy. The first concerns the covering of the skin with a hairy layer, composed of a multitude of vacuum-sealed solar tubes capable of gathering heat from solar energy; the second regards the appearance of growths on the surface which increase the possibility of generating energy as flexible photovoltaic panels in silicon.

Already in this project, then, the conviction is found that virtuous behaviors of architecture can be possible as long as they are conceived of as composed of elements in very great number, interacting with each other and with the environment, and as long as they use computational power to build a model capable of bringing the building closer to a true interactive system. In the case of *(Un)plug*, however, it goes further: the building that becomes autonomous can even disconnect itself from the urban network. The system closes energetically and this closure seems to correspond to the appearance of a troubled identity, that of an architecture which observes the *organization* of living systems with great interest.

2.6 Ecological Conspiracies Between Architecture and Living Beings

François Roche and N.T. thus seem to place the conviction that *perception, cognition, and experience*, in the words of Varela,

(UN)PLUG, LA DEFENSE, PARIS, 2001

The building that, becoming autonomous, can disconnect from the power supply corresponds to the appearance of a restless architectural identity, which looks with increasing interest at the living systems and their organizational closure.

A rendering of the urban integration of the project (top), models (bottom), and a diagram of the conceptual development (right).

Thompson, and Rosch, cannot be separated from each other (Varela, Thompson, and Rosch, 1991) at the center of their design experience founded in the information paradigm. In this light, information has a significance that goes well beyond its codification and de-codification through technical instrumentation. Acting as a new epistemology for the dialogue between living and artificial systems, information enables the reciprocal and multiple couplings between different systems, defining relations that make use of the environment in which they operate. The distinction between members of an environment, between artificial and living, thus loses its traditional classificatory value. This allows the architectural project to act as a new organism emerging from interactions with its environment, and co-participating in the cognitive, perceptive, and historical events that occur.

The proof of this reasoning is a project that converses with a site 51 whose critical components relate to the landscape, as a result of historical practices connected to agriculture and livestock and of peculiar geographical features. We are in Évolène in the Swiss Alps, where N.T. has a program that includes a farmhouse, a barn for cows, storage for hay, for wood, and space for beehives.

A theme so distant from those normally dealt with through Information Technology would lend itself to the immediate risk of vernacular temptation, or to the correct and peaceful interpretation of a critical regionalist approach. With *Scrambled Flat* there is, however, a reflection on information as the substance of a territorial condition, inextricably involved with the material and energetic components of the system under examination, and able to build sophisticated levels of relationship.

The key image offered by this project, which reasons along cycles relating to the use of resources in a co-participatory environment, is the sequence of seasonal variations of the shape of a sheaf of straw. It is an element that, as is conceivable, characterizes the landscape of the place and immediately recalls the presence of the cattle, the cycles that man has historically imposed on the environment, and the animals that have also ensured his survival. The sheaf, in fact, progressively diminishes in relation with the presence of livestock which it feeds during the winter. The cycle begins again when new hay is packed again by farmers in the summer, increasing the volume of the sheaf. This sequence of information, regarding the decrease and increase in interactions between living beings, restores the key to understanding the most basic needs that are able to co-exist with the environment.

Wood is considered to be the basic material of the small complex, consistent with traditional local technology based on it. Organic shells, superimposed but connected, are generated on the computer and cut in the facade by the plans of a parallelepiped with a pitched roof that forms the outer layer.

This silhouette, more than a reminder of the prevalent local typology, is the representation of information regarding the volume and surface
51 area used historically, as was done happened in the project for Venice. It is the opposite of what would be done through a landscape reading based on typology. The barn with cows is arranged on the ground floor, reserving the other spaces for humans and the bees. This results in an interstitial space between the shell aggregations and the outer volume. It is a void designed for the flows that arise from the presence of the bodies which inhabit the structure, where even the heat produced by the animals is considered to regiment the thermo-hygrometric conditions of comfort.

It precisely this *Boolean space* that N.T. considers crucial; it is, in fact, intended to be filled with hay and wood, thereby rooting the design in the traditional uses in Évolène. The hay accumulated in the interstitial space, which feeds the animals to the ground floor, also acts as an insulator in the winter. In the summer, however, when the animals are led to pasture, the hay will be nearly finished, resulting in open space which will be gradually filled up again with the approach of the winter season. The wood will follow the same cycle, being used in the winter to feed the fireplace and oven. The shells are entirely made of wood, and characterized by a continuity between the ground-floor and upper floors. They are connected by casings in an organic shape, using a complex climate control system that decodes and re-encodes the cycles which have existed for centuries in the place, through the information put into play in the system. It is a technique of conversation with the site, rather than detached observation that reads the landscape as an exclusive fact of memory. N.T., reinventing the context, doesn't disrupt its identity. If anything it is exactly the opposite, since the preservation of the identity of the context is achieved by learning from tradition, not imitating it in a sterile manner.

2.7 Against Memory and for Re-Creation
52-53 The evolution of *Scrambled Flat, Water Flux* of 2007, uses the same reasoning. The project is based on a program of activities including an art museum and a research station on the melting of glaciers. The

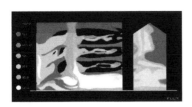

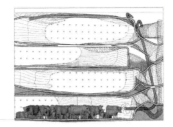

SCRAMBLED FLAT, EVOLENE, SWITZERLAND, 2001

A rural context, characterized by the direct relationship of humans and animals with the cycles of the seasons, is the basis of the project. Analyses of the flow of heat and sections of the small complex (top and right). The sequence of transformation from the sheaf of straw to the design idea (bottom left). Rendering of the project (bottom right).

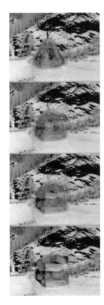

REGENERATING THE CONTEXT - WATER
FLUX, ÉVOLÈNE, SWITZERLAND, 2007

The cycle of glaciers is realized through the
materialization of latent information. The
regeneration of the environment does not concern
memory, but is rather the creative recognition of a fact
that is not only transmitted but which needs to be
recreated as happens in educational processes.

WATER FLUX

Rendering of the model (top right). Production of the wooden prototype through
processes of digital fabrication (center). Rendering of the building in the winter
(bottom).

WATER FLUX
The building participates in the seasons, freezing in the winter and creating a small pool of water through the thawing that occurs in the hot season. Rendering of the building in summer (top), and phases of processing of the wooden prototype through digital manufacturing processes (bottom left).

location is still the territory of Évolène, with the small village populated by about two thousand people. The surface, however, is approximately doubled. The key to the project is still in its ability to work with information focusing on the geographical history of the site; twenty years ago, in fact, the environment was completely different from the current one, because it was characterized by the presence of ice for most of the year. In the desire to restore this condition, not as a memory of the past to regret but as a latent and relevant identity, the building is equipped with a pool and a system capable of producing a small amount of artificial snow.

The outer casing is still parallelepiped with flaps, made with a grid attached to elements extruding from the wooden shells. Rooted in place, the wood comes from 50% of production, in two years, from the same village, thus even contributing to reactivating the local economy. The pieces are manufactured by a 5-axis CNC machine, and then are assembled and glued on the site. Some of the branches of the trees are preserved in the cutting, from which derives the spiny morphology of the architectural involucre.

Thus, in the winter season the snow completely covers the building, with the help of the snowmaking system, and, accumulating in the interstices, it transforms the building into a set of cavities and protuberances typical of the morphology of glaciers. In the warmer months, however, with the melting of ice the small pool is filled with water, once again changing the *ambience* of the building. It creates a closed loop tied to the study of glaciation. It is not, however, a staging of times gone by, but rather the repetition of a scientific experiment which, in agreement with the museum function, is able to involve the entire architecture. The glacial cycle becomes support for the snow: it is the regeneration of the environment through the materialization of latent information. There is no desire of memory, but instead the creative recognition of a fact that is not only transmitted, but which must be recreated and understood as occurs in real educational processes.

2.8 Unity Between the Living and Artificial: The Role of the Body
In examining N.T.'s projects the desire to rediscover architecture as a vital fact, not so much in its formal components as in its organizational, becomes increasingly clear. These are buildings that regard the corporeal world, its peculiar sensibilities, and the complexity of relationships that a body is able to establish with its environment until

the point that they can be considered together as a unit. A term that can explain this phenomenon, and which we have used, is *coupling*, a word that derives from cybernetics and cognitive science, and which emphasizes the relationships of interdependence that occur between agents, in terms of information or phenomenologies. According to some cognitive scientists, the environment is inseparable from the organisms that live in it and, more than a form of *background* information attained by them, is an integral part of a single system composed of organisms and the environment (thesis of *Radical Embodied Cognitive Science*).

According to this more radical approach computationalism in the explanation of the exchange of information, and thus of the cognitive acts that occur between different agents in an environment, should be rejected as the sole explanation.

In building an architecture that looks to the living and which is constituted as an environment, N.T. succeeds in attaining a multitude of approaches that reject mere computationalism but integrate it with the intelligence of a body. N.T. does not look to a single elaboration of information but to various possible forms, all underlying *protocols hidden in nature* among which the central is that of bodies.

2.9 Elephants Don't Play Chess
The awareness of creating order in an environment and, thus, usable information involves the search for hidden relationships and the establishment of unusual and unexpected links in the work of N.T. This leads the group to create mutual relationships between all the members of a community from which the meaning of the project literally emerges. Thus the division between artificial muscle, such as the steam engine, and natural muscle, mainly the tradition of having human or animal force, fades, because both can have the same value in creating more complex and specialized levels of information. This is what happens in the project *Hybrid Muscle* that N.T. created in 56 Thailand in 2003. The operation derives from the invitation of Philippe Parreno to Roche, to design a common space in which to live and create.

Parreno has the intention to use this space for the realization of a film, *The Boy from Mars*. The idea is that such a place, at the end of the process, can be used as a public and creative space by the local community. Roche sees an open/covered casing set on a static platform of concrete, using wood for the elevated structural part, and

HYBRID MUSCLE, CHANG MAI, THAILAND, 2003

The buffalo that grazes in the vicinity of the architecture is an integral part of its environment, but to be a part of this can also signify a distribution of its energy. The buffalo, in fact, can lift a large weight of metal, thus accumulating energetic potential in the structure.
When the weight falls down, the energy is released and becomes available. The pavilion with the buffalo (top). View of the interior and of the mechanisms that regulate energy storage (bottom from left to right).

elastomeric sheets for the covering. The bond of the operation is that, given the local conditions, the pavilion created should be self-sufficient, capable of producing energy without relying on supply networks which, furthermore, do not exist. How is it best to organize this energetic closure considering what already exists in the environment? The concepts elaborated for *Un(plug)* are subjected to a new challenge, being placed in a radically different location that that of urban Paris. In the case of the project in question here, the strategy 56 is to *couple* the small pavilion with a living being, first identified as an elephant and subsequently as an albino Thai buffalo. What is the crucial role of this animal? The buffalo grazing in the vicinity of the architecture is an integral part of its environment, but being a part of this can also mean a distribution of its energy. So, through a play of pulleys and cables which form an integral part of the project, it raises a two-ton weight of metal.

This, of course, in physics means to accumulate *potential energy*; when the weight falls down again, like an elastic mechanism, energy is released and can be used to charge ten power lamps and batteries for laptops and cell phones.

Other pneumatic mechanisms are not activated in the realized project, but would allow for the controlled opening of the sheets of elastomers in relation to climatic conditions. The architecture at this point is autonomous, and the buffalo can enjoy well-deserved rest before repeating the cycle.

Where does this small architecture begin? Does it begin from the threshold of the pavilion and the presence of the beast, without which it might not function? Within the rice field in which it is located this small structure, which has recently received the PAALMA (artist & architect 2009) award, seems to have provided its own version of sustainability. It has done this by proposing a coupling between a living beast and architecture in which the elephant/buffalo is used as an a-computational intelligence, essentially a body able to transfer energy. This is also good in generating information, and a more sophisticated order of uses and relations in the context in which it lives.

2.10 … But Robots, Yes (Do Play Chess)!

The point is that there is not only computational intelligence, which is programmable in computers, but that the presence of an organism, of an environment and its *features*, is also an informational resource. Robots, which were central to the experience of *I've heard about*, can

be considered the pinnacle of this crucial reasoning in Information
Technology. An optimal way to operate a robot, in fact, is to equip it
not only with a computer that forms it, oversimplifying *the mind*, but
also makes recourse to information that it can directly draw from its
physical conformation by its being situated in an environment. A
robot of this kind cannot only *play chess*, but may also be able to
execute tasks that will modify its physical environment. For this reason
59-60   the project for the competition for the extension of Frac Centre in
Orléans, named *Olzweg*, is one of the more significant works of Roche
and N.T., although already developed in 2006. What can a robot do
in architecture? And how is it possible to activate a new urban
environment in terms of processes rather than in terms of content?
What is the enormous contribution of N.T. in overcoming the
misunderstanding by which computer technology in architecture has
been confused with the appearance of the so-called *media building*?
The *Olzweg* project responds to many of these crucial questions,
serving as a sort of pragmatic manifestation of Information
Technology in architecture, like *I've heard about*, and certainly making
use of a good dose of sensible realism rather than the speculative
60   dimensions of the previous project. The expansion will be decided
within the existing courtyard. The environment to transform is
considered an information construction site, a space cognitively similar
to that of computers where the processing of information, the ability to
create new constructs, assemblies, and connections, determines a
permanent *work in progress* environment.

Thus, instead of designing an icon, N.T. proposes to couple a robot
with the existing museum, to be located in the courtyard in which the
new museum addition is expected. To better understand the role of this
robot we must observe that it is simultaneously a machine, in the
sense that it is able to produce work, and a cognitive agent, in the sense
that it is able to process information.

Its task is to recycle the glass produced in town and to literally use this
material to build the addition projected for the courtyard. The process
is anything but linear. The robot, through recycling, produces strips of
glass which are progressively stacked along the edges of the court until
they produce a new environment, thus assuming an eminently
constructive role. Once again, however, N.T. *dirties* the classic
cognitive model of the elaboration of information by substituting a
non-deterministic procedure for one which was formerly deterministic.
A deterministic procedure could, in fact, entail producing a

OLZWEG, PARIS, 2006

A permanent work in progress environment, subject to continuous upgrade, is created by coupling a robot with the existing architecture. Prototypes of the addition with the model of the robot, and internal view (left). Rendering of additions (center), and frames of the robot in motion (right). Diagrams of possible walking paths (bottom left).

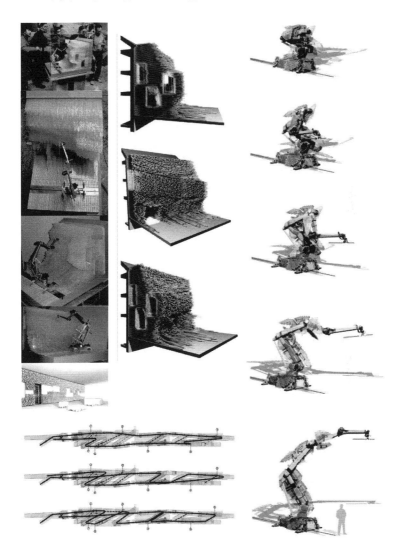

OLZWEG

The robot is designed as a controlling agent more than as a simple industrial machine. It can be considered a kind of cleaning fish, says Roche, which cleans one space thus bringing back another. The robot in action inside of the addition fabricated by the same (top). Simulation of the space obtained in the court after a certain number of robotic iterations (bottom).

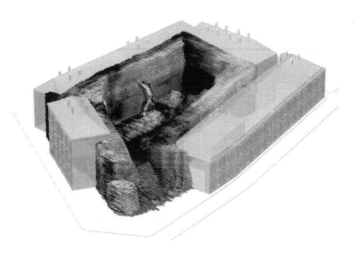

predetermined shape upstream from the process. The opposite of this conversely, is choosing a procedure able to include more and more reality, resulting in an architecture form which will emerge from the local contingencies.

The cognitive model actually used and the program that controls the behavior of the robot (technically a *scattering* script) are based on 59 stochastic models. Models of this type are those able to include the noise and unpredictability of certain real phenomena (for example, the passing of cars on a street). The addition is thus constructed introducing a level of *randomness* which results, in a process that would take about ten years, in a labyrinthine and phantasmagorical form that grows on the inner courtyard. The addition obtained is the result of a virtuous transformation achieved starting from the waste produced by inhabitants of the city, re-usable by the same people in the form of a museum thanks to the fundamental action of recycling performed by the robot.

In the *drift* of the bodies of situationist memory which, according to Roche, should occur in the museum experience, is inserted an element of self-control, giving visitors a PDA (Personal Digital Assistant) provided by RFID that allows them to orient themselves when they want to. The robot thus takes form as a *control agent* more than as a simple industrial machine. It can be considered a sort of *cleaning fish*, Roche tells us, which cleans one space and replaces it with another. The result of its action is not heteronomous, but is rather to reproduce the same environment in which it operates. The *destruction* and *reconstruction* of the components, in hindsight, is the main strategic use of robots in architecture, a strategy already evident at the protocol level in *I've heard about* that we can now identify more broadly with the processes of generation and regeneration of materials that occur in living systems.

2.11 And the Body?

Biological or robotic agents, with their unique aptitudes, thus become a catalyst in the design reasoning of N.T., and it is the organism or agent in the environment with its multiple relations that counts. It is the peculiarity of a relationship, emphasized and placed at the center of a building based on the processing of information, to inspire the creation of a scenario, and not vice-versa.

Another aspect, which should by this point be clear, is the role of corporeality between all of the components that Roche succeeds in putting into play. In these cycles everything seems to converge on the body as a natural or artificial cognitive agent that produces, uses, improves, and makes the architecture function. The project could not be thought of together with the bodily experience that is material, biological, and central in the architecture. This aspect is radicalized by Roche in another project that shows how it is possible to work in an ecological paradigm, while staying away from the reassuring categories of much *green architecture.*

Ecological thinking, in fact, regards the relationship between the body, its fluids, and environment, and this observation can form the basis for the design of a bar. These are dimensions that are certainly removed from the aseptic practice inaugurated by the hygienic protocols of standard modernists; between psychology and physiology, Roche and his group come to reassess corporeality in its dirtier dimensions. This bar is, in fact, a place where rather than leaving it, the users deposit their urine to then recycle and drink it. It is still necessary to highlight the possibility of a closed cycle, one which is certainly provocative and

63 even ironic, which shows how the themes of *transformation and the reabsorption of ones own liquids* (Roche 2007) may give rise to architecture.

The *Mi(pi)* bar, as it is called, was conceived as a swollen and unexpected outgrowth on one of the walls of the Wiesner Building of I.M.Pei at the MIT. It thereby caused a transfiguration of the sheer volume existing in a living body, supporting an already-established perception of the building which is known among students as Pei Toilet.

The outgrowth, articulated geometrically through *Voronoi* tessellation, is designed in inflatable materials with the insides covered in washable white leather. More than a waste product urine in this architecture is considered a *sterile* product that through gradual infusion, at times along with tea, can be reabsorbed by the body again, thus closing a cycle. The architectural environment is what allows this and articulates reabsorption, because it is within the outgrowth that the systems which allow the filtering and recycling are located. The result is a project that looks like an alchemical distillery, in which the yellow liquid is provocatively exhibited.

The reason for this space is the continuous tandem between bodily activities which are normally removed and relegated to a dirty area, and purifying and transformative actions of the architecture itself. The body and the architectural space are thus joined, creating a

MI(PI) BAR, MIT, WIESNER BUILDING - WORK IN PROGRESS (SINCE 2007)
The reason for this space is a continuous tandem between bodily activities normally removed
and relegated to a dirty area, and the purifying and transformative actions of the architecture
itself. The body and the architectural space are joined, giving rise to mutual co-existence.

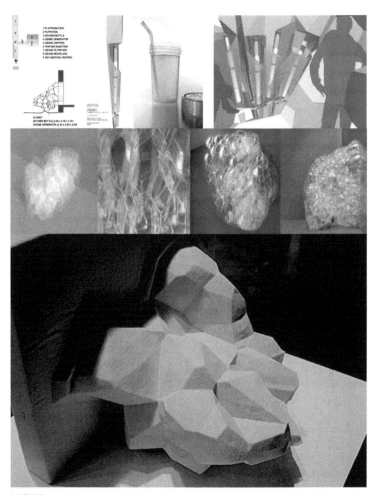

MI(PI) BAR
Study of the systems of filtration and purification of urine, and three-dimensional models of
Voronoi tessellation (top). Model of the bar emphasizing the nature of growth as
paradoxically generated from the pre-existing building (Wiesner Building).

mutualistic co-existence. Continuing an action similar to that already developed in the project *Aqua Alta 2.0*, a bar in Venice focused on the absorption of water purified from the lagoon, or that of the absorption of poisons proposed in *thegardenofearthlydelights*, N.T. expands the domains of bodily interaction with and within environments, even considering those which are most repugnant. A truly ecological architecture, it seems, can only start from these.

2.12 Co-evolution Between Architecture and the Environment
If the environment is not a chessboard, says Roche, and intelligence is not only computational, the dichotomy between nature and artifice is resolved in the reciprocal pairs that can be conceived and designed using the very phenomena of the living world. This is not hybridization, which is often a loss in identity, but the detection of relationships already existing in nature. In symbiosis, the organisms support one another and co-evolve within the environment that they contribute to define; the environment, in turn, evolves as a result of these elementary interactions. Order and complexity increase, as do the levels of interaction. The result is not a Darwinian competition for a few, but a mutual collaboration for many. If information becomes the main food in the understanding of these phenomena and in their restitution in models, computer technologies make them possible to implement. In 66 *Symbiosis' Hood*, a recent project, these concepts are pronounced. The site is still that of a boundary condition, the DMZ (the de-militarized zone) near Heyri in South Korea.
The program includes a residence with adjoining exhibition space, but for two separate owners of bordering plots. Again a negative bond, such as that relating to the distinction between proprieties, triggers a reasoning that culminates in a systemic organization. N.T. thus designs a building which consists of two arms which develop according to a helical movement, intertwined with one another and also involving the surrounding terrain which is consequently deformed. The form, then, is the result of a geometric model of symbiosis programmed and processed by the computer through a *twist movement* which organizes the possible response to the negative constraint of the boundary between the two properties.
The program of the building is then articulated according to two needs: light and vegetation, each offered by one of the two arms of the building and from the respective owner. One is transparent, the other used to purify the wastewater, entrusting its operation to the

experience gained in the projects that proposed hydroponic solutions. Symbiosis occurs also in the way functions are divided and benefit from 66 each other. Thus the public functions (including the exhibition space) are placed in the underground part, and in the extruding parts are the domestic spaces. The two arms of light and vegetation cling to each other, branching further and enabling functions conducted in a mutualistic manner. An ecologic strategy, therefore, generates the shape of the landscape.

To purify water, Roche chooses the Kudzu (*Pueraria Lobata*), a climbing species, infective and competitive, with the ability to engulf and destroy other plants. In the symbiosis, therefore, that which is painful and not peaceful always underlies the miraculous negotiations that occur in nature among living systems.

2.13 In Symbiosis with the Cosmos: Hyper-Architectural Research
The coincidence between the information and ecological paradigms and their convergence on the human being, pushes N.T.'s research at different cognitive magnifications to perform tasks that are full of meaning in contemporary architecture, and which involve at least two final achievements. The first is the extension of computational models from the abstract world of computer display to the material world, both man-made and natural, having sensed that these models can still work interactively in the physicality of architecture and in the dense contexts of history and life. The second, which is also a consequence of the first, is that the relationships provoked by these models can be built using not only electronic components, but also making use of the characteristics of matter, living or not. The relationship between model and reality thus becomes more correspondent and circular; one dimension *informs* the other, and vice-versa. This extension, which sees abstract and computational information intertwine with its *protocol of nature*, involves a continual openness of the architectural design. N.T. thus establishes a multi-dimensional architectural model which is at the same time mathematical, physical, psychological, and biological.

One of N.T.'s recent projects, *TheBuildingWhichNeverDies* (2009- 68-69 11), expresses this acquisition. The building was commissioned by Zumtobel, a corporation that deals with lighting, and is based on a functional program centered on research related to light, which is to be carried out in relation to various scientific hypotheses. A distinctive feature concerns the body, and more specifically the adaptation of the

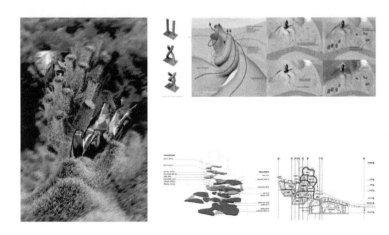

CO-EVOLUTION - SYMBIOSIS'HOOD, SEOUL, KOREA, 2009
The functional program includes a residence with adjoining exhibition space, but for two separate owners of adjacent plots of land. Again a negative constraint triggers reasoning which culminates in systemic organization. The symbiosis is organized both as a computational geometric procedure (the twist), and as the interactions between the functions and roles of the two arms. Rendering of the building embedded in the landscape (top and left). Generative diagram of the symbiosis and organization in elevation (bottom right).

human eye to darkness which must be studied in the laboratory This apparently negligible circumstance determines the construction of a chain of relationships that, starting from physiology, raises questions of astronomical nature and vice-versa. Consequently, in addition to the study of adaptation to the dark research should be carried out on the melatonin effect to test human metabolism relating to circadian cycles. Using OLED lamps and no more than an ecological mindset the research should also assess the weakness of the ozone layer. It works on a chain of multiple and non-linear causes, interrogating *the relationships* between living things and environments, but there is an additional step that is done in *TheBuildingWhichNeverDies,* which relates to the method.

Directly implicating human visual perception in relation to brightness, N.T. assumes as *basic information* the minimum illumination described by the relation 0.5 LUX equal to lunar light, by convention. This fact gives rise to an initial link between the building and the Moon, in the 68 sense that lunar light will be used as basic available information. This bond is translated architecturally through the correspondence between the local position of the building (in Les Andelys in France) and the position of the Moon on the Celestial Vault.

This is followed by another crucial condition: the building must maintain this correspondence in time, following the moon in its apparent motion. The architecture is then designed as a machinic system of gears at the base, designed on a plot of apparent motion across the sky. It is an architecture capable of rotating, tracing the longitudes on the xy-plane and adjusting the latitude in the xz-plane. Thus a microcosm is established, almost another celestial body, on the site. The information behind the project is therefore a spatial-temporal substance in a building that is perhaps the ideal continuation of the observatory of Mendelsohn in Berlin, almost a century later. The observatory-structure, in its appropriation of information on the astronomic scale, is further subjected to the action of the Coriolis forces that act on the four cardinal points relative to its position, which determine the shape of its whirling.

It is an attempt of formal genesis, which relies on information relevant to the physics of systems in play, and not on the metaphorical shift in lines, planes, and surfaces, of facts existing on the site.

The other relationship the building seeks to establish converges instead on the body: the swirling casing, in fact, is composed of several layers that act to filter and modulate the passages of light necessary for

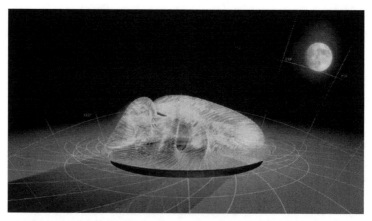

IN SYMBIOSIS WITH THE COSMOS - THEBUILDINGWHICHNEVERDIES, LES ANDELYS, FRANCE AND AUSTRIA, 2009-11

From the constraint of minimally perceptible light information, a chain of relationships is triggered between visual perception and building, between the building and the Moon. These chains create a building-observatory able to rotate and follow the celestial body, but also to reveal other phenomena that relate to the planetary scale. All reports converge on the physiology of the body of the user. Rendering of the building with its position in relation to the Moon (top). Top view and generative diagram (bottom).

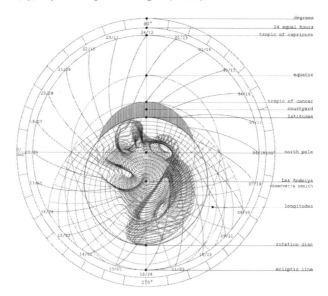

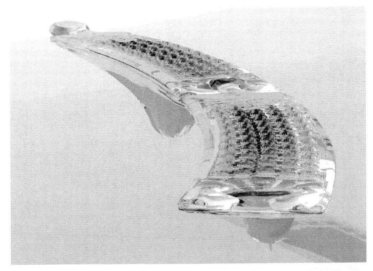

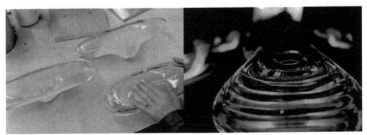

THEBUILDINGWHICHNEVERDIES

The building is covered by a photo-sensitive surface capable of giving negative information, that of UV radiation, not through electronic simulation but via the physical nature of the material. Elevation on the road of the laboratory (top). Realization of the first prototypes with Isobiot®ope for the outer covering (middle and bottom).

the perform the tests, managing, through different lens systems, to gradually tune out the light of the sun. In such a tunnel a flash of 0.5 LUX is emitted, which allows for the execution of tests on the conditions of minimum perception. The morphology of the building, therefore, is affected by this concomitant reciprocity. The bodily interactions are further explored in the research on melatonin production and its implications on circadian rhythms, correlating to the levels of brightness of the devices produced by Zumtobel.

With regard to the studies concerning the presence of UV radiation and the problem of ozone depletion, the relationship with the body expands further and ends by being considered in its more pathological dimensions as well. Roche thus also makes his architecture a marker of the presence of danger. Inventing a special material, the Isobiot®ope, whose components are mineral powders capable of producing radioactive emissions (phosphorescence), he covers the skin of the building with photovoltaic cells and glass plates in which this material is lodged. By absorbing UV radiation it is able to return intensity in the form of flashes that are released during the night following day-time absorption. In this way a photosensitive surface is obtained, which is capable of returning negative information through the intimate nature of the material used, rather than from electronic simulation. A prototype based on the Isobiot®ope was presented at the Venice Biennale in 2010. The *abstract machine* by Von Neumann and the *analogous machine* by McCulloch, two antithetical but consubstantial visions in the History of Information Technology, finally meet together: information is linked to the physics of materials, and they couple definitively. But to discuss this affirmation thoroughly we need to move from an associative logic of information to an organizational one.

2.14 Constructive and Destructive Architectural Machines

To organize information not only to produce symbolic models of the city or territory, but rather to build relationships, behaviors, dynamic equilibria, energetic exchanges, and new materials, is the most evident contribution of N.T. to architecture conceived in the information paradigm. To organize processes of this kind, that are able to bring architecture closer to the world of the living, should, in hindsight, not signify only construction but also destruction. To understand this concept thoroughly, we need to analyze the design of a pavilion whose main purpose is to dissolve into its environment or, in other words, to self-destruct. It is the continual death of cells that allows the renewal of tissues, and in Roche's research this theme, already embryonic in the project *I've heard about*, is directly treated in the installation *Things which necrose* (2009-10). The pavilion, in water-soluble plastic ⁷² obtained from materials derived from agricultural activities, is made with a 5-axis CNC machine. Necrosis, the process of progressive tissue destruction, is induced through a controlled administering of water particles by means of humidifying nozzles. It processes information regarding the level of humidity in the tissues, and manipulates it to materially provoke the dissolution of the material.

The prototype is made as if it were the magnification of a porous tissue, also equipped with a series of ciliary protrusions that guide the water as if they were drippers. With this pavilion of exceptional importance N.T. indicates a change in the state of architecture which, from constructive art par excellence, becomes *transformative* art. *Construction and destruction* can be understood, therefore, as extreme terms of a process of transformation which N.T. explores fully. On one side there is architecture which is able to self-build as in *I've heard about*, and on the other there is architecture that can also self-destruct. At the end of its life cycle, Roche seems to say, the building can dissolve into its own environment like living systems that have contributed to the ecological history of the planet.

Things which necrose also seems to close a cycle with respect to the long journey that computer technology has meant for architecture; from a logic relating to abstract information processed from a computational and symbolic point of view, a methodology of the re-appropriation of nature's own protocols is attained, which organizes information according to the relationships that occur between matter, whether inert or living.

THINGS WHICH NECROSE, DENMARK, 2009, SUEDE, 2010

The pavilion is made of water-soluble plastic. Necrosis, the process of progressive tissue destruction, is then induced through the management of controlled humidity, implemented by some nozzles. The building, at the end of its life cycle, can dissolve into its environment like living systems.

THINGS WHICH NECROSE

A model placed within the environment (top left). Samples of material and prototype (top right). Study of the tissue and porosity (lower left). Sills in the prototype (bottom right).

3. Towards an Architecture as a Living System

3.1 The Project of New-Territories as a Strategy for Living Architecture
What characterizes a living system such as this, according to Maturana and Varela, is the existence of two crucial conditions. The first is that the components of the system are related to each other according to a closed organization, although they are still open to crucial and determining exchanges to guarantee its survival. The second is that these components have the capacity to *destroy themselves and regenerate*, thus preserving the *identity* of the system. It is the continuous processes of *destruction and construction* that occur in a living system (Maturana and Varela 1985) that mark the difference between a simple machine, such as an industrial one, and a *living machine*. If the interactions of N.T.'s projects are designed to *be open to all transactions* (Roche 2005), it is certain that crucial element which is the body, user, and organism, that reiterates for the architecture its destiny of coexistence. A recent study of N.T., *An Architecture "des humeurs,"* presented to the eponymous exhibition of Le Laboratoire in Paris in 2010, interweaves these strands again and repeats the coupling between architecture and body according to the different dimensions that relate to the exchange of information, until it also includes those more intangibly related to feelings. In the exhibition, the public is invited to take part in an immersive protocol that, through touch and biofeedback, returns information through the organism's release of molecules such as dopamine, adrenaline, serotonin, and cortisol. The technology developed by a large team of researchers involves the use of steam in which nano-particles are released that, when inhaled, allow, in exhalation, the balancing of the levels of these molecules "of humor" present in the organism. This information has to do with the animal nature of the body according to which Roche is able to deny human language. It is used in a *bottom-up* process to condition the constructive logic of architecture that becomes a morphology of the living part of the body, resulting from the moods of the individual and of the multitudes in relation to each other. Of the robots employed the VIAB02 builds the structure through the secretion of bio-cement, responding to the logic of an algorithm that calculates and optimizes the trajectories in real time as influenced by the stimuli of the inhabitants. What emerges is a complex that responds to a logic which is opposed to the top-down logic of collective settlements; it is a logic that is open to the mystery of bodily secretions, to the contradictory

complexity of living machines, and to the multidimensionality of the information that they process. In some ways the project can also be considered a concrete evolution on parts of the protocol of *I've heard about. An Architecture "des humeurs,"* then, outlines a new dimension to the old problem of identity in architecture, overturning the links and promoting the biology of the body as the basis of production of the self and thus of cognition, as the sole characteristic which is able to promote *identity* as a cultural aspect of architecture. Never have so many fundamental experiences of the twentieth century, from psychoanalysis to phenomenology, from physics to information technology, been problematized and summarized in an architectural project.

3.2 An Architecture that is Self-Produced

Joining with living systems, then, the architecture which is seen in the work of N.T. continuously expands its functional, performative and semantic domains, ultimately arriving at the real possibility of creating the conditions for its *self-production*.

To use another term from Maturana and Varela, it is an architecture that is *autopoietic*, organized according to a system which is physically closed and identifiable but, and most of all from the point of view of the information and exchange, open to all possible negotiations. It is a living system, precisely.

3.3 Information, Energy, and Matter

The research that Roche and N.T. deliver to this stage of the Information Revolution concerns not only the role of technology within a discipline – architecture – which is by its own nature transformative, but also the membership of architecture as a disciple in the information paradigm according to an inclusive logic that converges on the human being. Information, energy, and matter, which contemporary scientific research not surprisingly tends to consider convergent, refer only to different descriptions of the same reality. The hopes of cybernetics, regarding information as a new science able to open further dimensions of interaction in all sensible reality, have not gone up in smoke.

Gre(Y)en

by François Roche

(a history of local operative criticism)

... that seems to pretend to be a history of stuttering position between
Green and Grey, between chlorophyll addiction, dream of an ideal
biotope, re-primitivized, re-artificialized, in the pursuit of the lost
paradise, of the lost Eden Park, as a story for little boys and girls, for
sleeping their fears and ... the Grey, the deep grey, which never
appears in the visible spectrum ("The greatest *trick* the *devil* ever
played was convincing the world that he did not *exist*.", said
Baudelaire) as an antagonism stealth forces, an embedded demon:
mixture of contradictory human desires emerging from the mud, from
permanent, unpredictable and irreducible conflicts, factor of
domination and servitude, destruction and emergences, which are
fireworking an unlimited source of arrogance and illusion, where the
notion of success and failure are depending on a kind of absurd
Pendulum of life and death, caressing the boundaries of the both, as an
infinite unstable movement, polymerizing ugliness and beauty,
obstacle and possibilities, of waste materials and efflorescence, of
threats and protection, of technological phantasm and revenge of
nature, in a knot, in the process of becoming, a never-ending
movement ... where we glide into this silky, strange sensation that
scares you and caresses you ... That scares you and caresses you ...
We are at the crossroads, where, faced with the autistic, blind, deaf and
mute violence of our mechanisms of technological, industrial,
mercantile and human servo-mechanism, nature reacts ... with
violence and without warning, in a faltering of the original chaos ... in
mutiny against the organization of men ... Gaïa seems to take revenge
(Katrina, El Niño, Cyclone Jeanne, Tomas and Nargis, the Xynthia
storm, Ewiniar typhoon, Indonesian and Japanese earthquakes,
collateral Tsunamis all the way to Fukujima ... chain of devastating
incertitude, unpredictable in spite of our seismographic sciences). The
elements rage and the gods, so quick to pardon our folly, seem
powerless to appease the rebellion, armed with infernal force ...
Nature is not an ideological "green washing" for backyard politics, nor
the millenarian, eschatological dream of Eden Park, from which we
have very fortunately escaped, freeing ourselves from the gatherer-

hedonist blindness, to negotiate consciousness with the hostile dark
forces that get stuck, in the depths of the forest ...
But these forces have come out of their hiding places, their biotopes,
they are invading the spaces that Man had thought he could take
without giving anything in exchange, without transaction ... the war
has been declared ... nature's revenge is not a bedtime story for
innocent brains ... our bellicose enemy operates openly ... in the light
of day ... ultimate arrogance ...
How could we reveal the conflict between the strategies of "knowledge
and domination" of the first and the monstrous wild beauty of
destruction of the other ... as the field of an unpredictable battle,
disconnected, cleared of all the greenish moralism jumble and its post-
capitalism lure ...
To help to feel this ambivalence, this permanent disequilibrium, where
contingencies are the main factor of emergences, let us navigate in this
history of *gre(Y)en.*
... From a physiological early simple dualism *shadow & light* in 1990,
where Neuschwanstein Grotto is f®ictionally adjusted to Play-Time
mirror refection, weakly connecting a cavernous, dark, humid,
sensorially primitive atmosphere with its schizophrenical antagonist
twin brother, crystalline, cold, luminous, dry, technologically blind as
the recognition of an impossible stuttered dialogue, to .... a *Growing
up* for a chlorophyll energy and entropy in 1993 that will collapse and
strangle a fragile "chicken legs" house, wrapped and dominated
masochistically by the danger of its own predictable death if the
maintenance is not ritualized by the owner as a permanent conflict
against the destructive strength and his needs to survive ... to a blur
petrochemical *Filtration* in 1997, with 5,000 m^2 of plastic stripes floating
in the tree, on the edge of a seasonal tidy wild river, carrying nitrate and
insecticide plastic bag residues that the farmer abandoned on the bank
of their field, waiting for this rising up for a depolluting natural service,
in charge of erasing the trace of their chemical addiction, and
paradoxically back to the visible spectrum when the river is down
again, hanging from the branches. The "Filtration" layer reveals by the
concentration of the plastic wasted in the canopies an aesthetic
countryside planning coming directly from its human managing ... to
travel to the weird ... *aqua alta1.0,* in 1998, sucking up the disgusting,
viscous, over-polluted liquidity called the Venetian Lagoon, to use
capillarity's water forces of the contaminated to infiltrate literally, the
building emergences from these lagoon substances, to ... *aqua alta 2.0,*

the Venetian bar in 2000 at the Architectural Biennale of Venice, where "conventioneers" could refresh themselves by drinking "in live" the lagoon soup, but depolluted through a military purification machine to test in the condition of the Biennale; the schizophrenia between green washing rhetoric discourse and repulsive digestive paranoia on the doubt of the reliability of the cleaning engine, which people promote as efficient technologies (for the others) ... to *shearing* in 2001, as a simple stealth private House, organizing a simulacrum of its own impermanency and apparent fragility, unfold in the countryside, but using for the whole envelope the authorized petrochemistry non-biodegradable fabric that is spread and disseminated in nature to preserve planted young trees from destruction by rabbits, in an agriculture industrial logic ... to *Dustyrelief*, in 2002, for the contemporary Art Bangkok museum where the dust of the city and the residue of the traffic jam (Dioxide and Monoxide of Carbon) dressed her skin and her biotope, as the recognition of public transportation failure in the "greynish" equatorial erotism, where this special fog of specks and particles becomes the traces of hypertrophic human convulsing activity, as a second adaptive nature, through a bottom-up unpredictable unmastering unplanning city aesthetic. Without delegating the power to autocratic and aseptic technocratic experts at the place of the chaotic emergences of the multitudes, the aleatory rhizomes, the arborescent growth are at the same time a factor of her transformation and her operational mode. The non-hygienic intoxicating urban chaos is the sign of its human vitalism, as a permanent vibe between Eros and Tanatos ... the invisible but breathable substances are bred, attracted by an electrostatism machine to "skin" the hairy freak, exacerbating a schizo climate between indoor (white cube and labyrinth in Euclidian geometry) and outdoor (dust relief on topologic geometry) ... and ... and in a second step collecting the particle substances, dropped down in the monsoon period, through drainage systems ... to create on the side the tea pavilion extension directly coming from the compacted particles brick produced "by" the failure and the beauty of the city ... to the ... *mosquitosbottleneck* scenario, in Trinidad, 2002, trying to negotiate with the infestation of the Nile Virus carried by Mosquitoes, for the recognition of this disease as an objective paranoia triggering strategies for safety, in a week-end residential house. The fragile net, through a Klein bottle apparatus, preserves, protects, but also disjoins the living of the first in resonance with the death of the other. And the sound of their agony, buzzing in the double trapped membrane, becomes the proof of the efficiency of the system, preserving human against nature, against its offensive non-inoffensive biotope, protected and surrounded by the theatre of its own barbaria ... to the buffalo Machismo no-tech Machinism in *HybridMuscle* in 2003, Thailand, as a local mammal muscling power station, lifting with gears of a two-ton steel counterweight, transformed in a battery house, transformed first in electricity plugs and connections and secondly in pneumatic rubber muscles movement of leaves in elastomer membrane to wind the suffocatingly hot sweaty climate ... as an endogeneous-exogeneous story telling ... to the *greengorgon*, in 2005, as a phasmid morphologies, embedded in a wood, which feeds the confusion between artificial and domesticated nature, where all the outdoor surfaces are dedicated to vertical wet swamp recycling the inert grey water ... as a purification plan infrastructure, rejecting only clean liquidities in the Leman lake ... to the *Mipi*, in 2006, a PI Bar in the temple of cognitive science, the MIT-Cambridge, as an extension of the Media Lab, to experiment through a urine therapy absorption, the immunotherapy of the individual human production, including a schizoid balance between disgusting and healthy effect ... to a stochastic machine that vitrifies the city, in *Olzweg*, 2006, starting the contamination from a radical architecture museum in the pursuit of Frederick Kiesler endlessnesslessness. This smearing is done through the industrial glass recycling (mainly French wine bottles), swallowed and vomited through a process of staggering, scattering and stacking by a 12-metre.high machine. The random aggregation is a part of this unpredictable transformation, as a fuzzy logic of the vanishing point. The machine works to extend the museum and collect "voluntary prisoners" wrapped in the permanent entropy of the graft, testing the glass maze through its multiple uncertain trajectories, to lose themselves and rediscover this heterotopian non-panoptical sensation of their youngness, using if necessary PDA on RFID to rediscover their positioning ... at the opposite of an architecture that petrifies, historicizes, panopticalizes ... to the *waterFlux* in 2007, for a scenario scooping out hollows in a full wood volume by a 5-axis drilling machine with 1,000 trees (2,000 m^3) coming directly from the maintenance of the forest around the location of extracting-manufacturing-transformation, as an anthroposophic logic, where technologies and machine are territorialized from the site, endemic to a situation and its mutation, reactivating accessorily local forest economy ... to the *gardenofearthlydelights,* in 2008, a toxic garden in a new green house in Croatia, on the right place of the initial middle-age Apotiker Franciscan monks medical plantation, protected behind a restricted area, but able to be tasted and tested through a distillation deconcentration machinism processes, and bar ... only by voluntary desire, in a similar way to the Japanese "Fugu" physiological and psychological effects ... with an "at your own risk" protocol, and where ecosophy is considered a global interaction, porous to human body, as Gaïa exchanges, a chain of interaction and dependences ... articulating life and death and its knitting paranoia ... to *Heshotmedown,* in 2008, for a tracked biomass machine penetrating into the (de)Military Zone, the DMZ, between North and South Korea, collecting the rotten substances, the superficial coating of the forest in decomposition, and bringing back this material to plug all the external surfaces of the ballistic-like building, for a natural eco-insulation, through the fermentation of the grass and the heat coming from its chemistry transformation. Full of land mines, the DMZ is a restricted zone, where North and South never stop to play the Cold War. The machine collects the ingredients of this pathological period and recycles them for productive use, from a highly dangerous no man's land abandoned since the end of the war (more than half a century ago), which come back to its natural wildness, with the reappearing of elves, wizards, witches and harpies, and some new vegetal species. Legends and fairy tales are transported out of the deepness of the forest, as in a "Stalker" experiment to touch the unknown ... to *I'mlostinParis,* in 2008, as a laboratory for bacterial culture, called the "Rhizobium" agent cultivated in 200 beakers, for its potential to increase the Nitrogenize per cent without chemical manure of the substract of each plant, after the re-injection of these substances in the individual nutritional aeroponic system ... for a "Rear windows" minimum distance to the conservatism and "petite bourgeoisie" of Parisian neighbourhoods, on the opposite views on closed courtyards ... this Devil's Rock emergence is constituted by 2000 ferns coming from the Devonian period and technologically domesticated to survive in the actual "regressive monarchic French period"... to a paranoiac system, the *TbWnD (the building which never dies)* in 2011, as an alert detection or a marker of our past/future symptoms: a Zumtobel laboratory on "dark adaptation" and on solar radiation intensity detection, covered by phosphorescent components *("Isobiot®opic" oxide pigment made from raw uranium)* working as a UV sensor and

detector to indicate and analyze the intensity of the UV rays that
touched the area by day (including on humans and all other species).
5000 glass components reveal the depletion of the ozone concentration
in the stratosphere and simultaneously the origin of this phenomenon,
the sun's radiation. This Lab articulates the risk coming from the
Ozone weakness (industrial pollution / CO_2) combined with the
paranoia coming from the last Century of scientific ignorance or
criminality, developed by the exploitation of the characteristic of some
natural element... to several escaping, coming first through a utopian
protocol the _an architecture des humeurs_ , in 2011, with a self-
organized urbanism conditioned by a bottom-up system in which the
multitudes are able to drive the entropy of their own system of
construction, their own system of "vivre ensemble", Based on the
potential offered by contemporary bio-science, the rereading of
human corporalities in terms of physiology and chemical balance, to
make palpable and perceptible the emotional transactions of the
"animal body", the headless body, the body's chemistry, and inform
about individuals' adaptation, sympathy, empathy and conflict, when
confronted with a particular situation and environment ... to adapt the
"malentendus" of this result to an endless process of construction
through "machinism" undeterminism and unpredictable behaviour
with the development of a secretive and weaving machine that can
generate a vertical structure by means of extrusion and sintering (full-
size 3D printing) using a hybrid raw material (a bio-plastic-cement)
that chemically agglomerates to physically constitute the
computational trajectories. This structural calligraphy works like a
machinism stereotomy comprised of successive geometrics according
to a strategy of permanent production of anomalies ... with no
standardization, no repetition, except for the procedures and
protocols, at the base of these technoid slum emergences ... and ... at
last but not least for the last experiment, the *hypnosisroom* in 2006
(Paris) and 2012 (Japan) ... using hypnosis cession for the stargate
effect, in the pursuit of the Somnambulist feminine political
movement, from the first half of the 19th century, using hypnosis
(called magnetism at this period) for an attempt to develop spaces of
freedom, egalitarian unracial, unsexist social contract, which could not
be perceived and explored without travelling through this layer ... at
the opposite of the impossibility (or difficulties) to modify the
mechanisms of the real, tangible, political state of the world ... this
prefeminist movement strove, on the contrary, to create this

suggestive, immersive and distanced layer of another social contract ...
Although diabolized and treated as charlatanism, nevertheless all of
premodern reformist thought drew on this movement ... and ...
End of the first chapter ...

Notes

The verses "Mes chers frères, n'oubliez jamais, quand vous entendrez
vanter le progrès des lumières, que la plus belle des ruses du diable est
de vous persuader qu'il n'existe pas." refer to: Charles Baudelaire, *Le
spleen de Paris* (1869).
Refer to Edgar Allen Poe, *The Pit and the Pendulum* (1842) as the first
scenario of Bachelor Machines.
Neuschwanstein Castle (1886). The palace, with its romantic artificial
grotto, was commissioned by Ludwig II of Bavaria as a retreat and as
an homage to Richard Wagner.
Playtime (1967), a film by Jacques Tati, with its glass-cold-deterriolised
futuristic urbanism.
A machine using both ozone and a ceramic system to create drinkable
water, without giving the Italian authorities the right to call it "Natural
Venice Water" is mentioned in the description of *Aqua alta2.0* project.
For WaterFlux, refer to the transcription from a lecture on the location
of the building-2012.
*This scenario in Switzerland is located in La Fauchère near Evolène
(waterFlux). The building will be erected at around 1,500 metres above
sea level in a mountainous area where – 20 years ago – the location was
covered by a glacier. It will look somewhat like a cocoon and be made
entirely of wood. A five-axis drilling machine will scoop out hollows
within the wooden volume as if it were an ice cavity. So you could say
that one natural element, the glacier, will be substituted by another
natural element, the pine. We want to understand how we can cut the
material and how we can shape the architecture by extracting, by cutting
out through a sophisticated technological process of transformation
that uses the material directly from the situation. The building is
monstrous in a way, like a Rabelaisian building – talking about this
chimera or this kind of stuttering between existing nature, primitive
nature and how the technology could transform them both. So we intend
to log trees from the nearby forest with a machine and bring the wood to
a village at the bottom of the mountain. For this project, we are not*

designing a special machine, but are using a tremendous computer-driven CNC machine. So we will come back with roughly 180 elements, each of them unique, and will reassemble them on site, as a topological Lego, with branches outside to maintain the illusion of the snow in a warming environment period to a topological shape similar to the melting ice cavern, indoors, as the dilemma of the glacier disappearing, as a schizophrenia.

The Val d'Hérens, the valley where Evolène is located, is a region with potential seismic activity, with earthquake risk, so we are also trying to invent a way to project this dangerousness onto the building: But in fact we reinforce in appearance the fragility of the multiple stacking elements in equilibrium. The wood we are using is absorbing through the variation of its thickness, depending on its location in the building, the structures, the insulation, the waterproofing. Some of the indoor spaces are frozen at -10 °C, like an attempt to keep the frozen fragments of a lost paradise, "what was the Alpine mountain" before the changing of climate, as a sanctuary. As usual in Swiss projects, the architect has to convince the people to avoid a petition against it. So last year I was in front of 1,500 people, and the mayor predicted to me that it will be my last day in the village. But I came with a mask, this kind of pagan mask that local people traditionally wear at the "Mardi Gras" (Fat Tuesday) carnival, to historically exorcise the winter period and welcome in the vitality of spring. They wear masks, they scream, they even beat each other up in the street, in a multitude of Bibendum Michelins, filled by grass in a hessian fat suit, running through the streets, as a ritual, as a ceremony of grotesque medieval behaviour. So before the voting, I justified the building insofar as it could exorcise global warming, testing a line of illogical and subjectivities to argue and articulate the monstrous design. And surprisingly, people, all from this mountain, reacted strangely positively and collectively adopted this interpretation as a plausible one, confusing the mask, the exorcising, and the design ... with a high degree of logic and lack of logic. I was in this case the ideal architect speaking about science but in a pataphysical way, articulating the true and the false, the reason and the madness and mainly the forbidden, where ghosts, witches, wizards, and yetis of the mountains were part of the common sharing of knowledge.

Gaïa hypothesis mentioned in the text, is a biogeochemical scientific possibility that the Earth should be a dynamic physiological system, including the biosphere, designed to maintain, for the past 3 billion years, the planet in harmony with life.

Stalker (1979), is a film by Andrei Tarkovskiy with a kind of post-war interzone, to across with a protocol, a ritual which has to be stickily followed, as the main condition to avoid waking up the forces nobody knows.

Rear Window (1954), is a film by Alfred Hitchcock, about voyeurism, relationships within a neighbourhood location, phantasms and realities ...

Devil's Rock, in the USA, was used by Steven Spielberg as the location platform for an alien gathering point, in his film *Close Encounters of the Third Kind* (1977). It was reproduced by Richard Dreyfus in the movie, in his own living room.

In the description of *The building which never dies*, we refer to the discovery of the property of the radium by Pierre and Marie Curie to the Plutonium day after-effect of the Little Boy bomb.

Moltitudes and *bottom-up* refer to Spinoza's and Antonio Negri's works.

Malentendu the word used in the description of an *architecture des humeurs* is a French word that navigates between mishearing and misunderstanding.

Bibliography and Further Reading

To build critical thought within research that is still fully in development I used primarily the following texts, for the ability of the authors to describe the technical and conceptual problems that computing entails, and their meaning in architecture. The dates refer to the edition I consulted, which in some cases was translated into Italian years after the publication in the original language.

Wiener 68 - Norbert Wiener, *Introduzione alla cibernetica l'uso umano degli esseri umani*, Universale Bollati Boringhieri, Torino 1968.

Saggio 07 - Antonino Saggio, *Introduzione alla Rivoluzione Informatica in Architettura*, Carocci, Roma 2007.

Wölfflin 10 - Heinrich Wölfflin, *Psicologia dell'Architettura*, et al/edizioni, Milano 2010.

Deleuze e Guattari 02 - Gilles Deleuze e Félix Guattari, *L'Anti Edipo. Capitalismo e schizofrenia*, Einaudi, Torino 2002.

Foucault 08 - Michel Foucault, *Sorvegliare e punire. Nascita della prigione*, Einaudi, Torino 2008.

Vidler 06 - Anthony Vidler, *Il perturbante dell'architettura. Saggi sul disagio nell'età contemporanea*, Einaudi, Torino 2006.

Corbellini 09 - Giovanni Corbellini, *Bioreboot. The Architecture of R&Sie(n)*, Architectural Press, New York, Princeton 2009.

Thompson 06 - D'Arcy Wentworth Thompson, *Crescita e Forma. La geometria della natura*, Universale Bollati Boringhieri, Torino 2006.

AD 10 - *It's in your nature: I'm lost in Paris*, «Architectural Design»,Vol. 80 n. 3, Special Issue: Territory: Architecture Beyond Environment, 2010 (essay by Javier Arbon).

AD 08 - *Bodies without organs* - Bwo, «Architectural Design», Vol. 78 n. 6, Special Issue: Neoplasmatic Design, 2008 (essay by François Roche).

AD 10 - *(Science) Fiction, Ecosophical Apparatus and Skizoid Machines*, «Architectural Design», Vol. 80 n. 6, 2010 (essay by François Roche).

Mouvement 10 - *Molecular Interfaces*, «Mouvement», Special Issue to n. 54, 2010 (essay by Jeanette Zwingerberger).

Sini 09 - Carlo Sini, *L'uomo, la macchina, l'automa. Lavoro e conoscenza tra futuro prossimo e passato remoto*, Bollati Boringhieri, Torino 2009.

Licata 08 - Ignazio Licata, *La logica aperta della mente*, Codice Edizioni, Torino 2008.

Morris 05 - Morris, R., Tarassenko L. and M. Kenward, *Cognitive Systems: Information Processing Meets Brain Science*, Elsevier Academic Press, San Diego CA 2005.

Piattelli Palmarini 08 - Massimo Piattelli Palmarini, *Le scienze cognitive classiche: un panorama*, Einaudi, Torino 2008.

Putnam 93 - Hilary Putnam, *Rappresentazione e Realtà. Il computer è un modello adeguato della mente umana?*, Garzanti, Milano 1993.

Chemero 09 - Anthony Chemero, *Radical Embodied Cognitive Science*, MIT Press, Cambridge, MA 2009.

Varela 91 - Varela, F. J., E. Thompson and E. Rosch, *The Embodied Mind. Cognitive Science and Human Experience*, MIT Press Cambridge, MA 1991.

Maturana e Varela 85 - Umberto Maturana, Francisco Varela, *Autopoiesi e cognizione. La realizzazione del vivente*, Marsilio, Venezia 1985.

Von Baeyer 05 - Hans Christian Von Baeyer, *Informazione. Il nuovo linguaggio della scienza*, Edizioni Dedalo, Bari 2005.

Brooks 90 - *Elephants Don't Play Chess*, «Robotics and Autonomus System», n. 6, MIT Artificial Intelligence Laboratory, Cambridge, MA, 1990 (essay by Rodney Allen Brooks).

Giolito 07 - Barbara Giolito, *Intelligenza Artificiale. Una guida filosofica*, Carocci, Roma 2007.

Capra 05 - Fritjof Capra, *La rete della vita*, BUR, Biblioteca Universale Rizzoli, Milano 2005.

Pallasmaa 05 - Juhani Pallasmaa, *The Eyes of the Skin: Architecture and the Senses*, Wiley-Academy, Chichester 2005.

The site New-Territories.com (http://www.new-territories.com) deserves special mention, for which I would like to emphasize the simple set-up and incredible generosity in content. Other articles and texts studied are directly available on this site. To deepen certain paragraphs of the book, I propose the following bibliographical notes and additions:

1. A Critical Position: Reconcilable Dualities Between Machines and Living Entities

N.T.'s criticism moves between positions derived from the thought of Roche himself, and in particular from his descriptive *protocols* and critical-philosophical constellation that draws on the thought of J. Lacan, De Sade, G. Deleuze, but also P. Sloterdijk and T. Negri. Of great interest, this criticism highlights the experience of N.T. in its political aspects, at the cost of its methodological and specific aspects, in relation to Information Technology. *AntiEdipo*, the first part of *Capitalismo e schizofrenia*, written by Deleuze and Guattari (translated in Italy in 1975), was, before an essay on liberation, a passionate polemic against one of the most important thinkers of the twentieth century, Sigmund Freud, and against psychoanalysis. Deleuze and Guattari sought to expand the idea of the subconscious, proposing a perspective that centered on the revolutionary character of desire. On the one hand, the polemic is connected with the *oedipal scene*, reduced by Freud to a small theater in which is staged nothing more than a family drama which is more than two millennia old. On the other hand, the alternative to the affective model of the oedipal triangle proposed is that of the *schizoid*, bearer of a subconscious considered as *desire production*.

Only for this reason can it give rise to a revolutionary potential whose release could overwhelm the repressive structures that determine its pathological state.

Deleuze, however, was also the philosopher of the *Fold*, another text of great literary charm despite its complexity. Beginning from *Folding*, on which the best architects of the first phase of the Information Revolution wrote repeatedly, and continuing with the concept of *Rizhoma*, the reference to Deleuze seems to have accompanied, perhaps to legitimate it, the discourse on the presence of information in architecture.

For the evolution of these concepts, consult the essays in this series, which reconstitute an interpretively and methodologically varied landscape. Deleuze, in addition to defining philosophy fundamentally as an activity giving rise to new concepts, was also one of the first philosophers to attempt a reading of art and science united under the creative activity of philosophy itself. It was also Deleuze to discover Gilbert Simondon, one of the first philosophers to attempt a systematization of information, a critique of cybernetics, and a concept of the machine.

For this, consult Gilbert Simondon (2011), *L'Individuazione alla luce delle nozioni di forma e informazione*, Vol. I and II (Mimesis Edizioni, Milano-Udine), edited by G. Carrozzini. In this text we have chosen an approach which is more consubstantial with the methods, tools, and methodological questions posed by Information Technology. A further avenue to explore, however, could be that between the thought of Roche and Guattari of the *Tre Ecologie* (Guattari 1989).

1.1 New-Territories.com: New Territories for Heretical Scenarios
For the concept of *logical openness*, one of the main threads of this book, see Licata (2008), pp. 178-189. With regard to the theory of Information dealt with from the engineering point of view, but also important from the conceptual point of view, reference is made to the well-known paper by Shannon, C.E. (1948), *A Mathematical Theory of Communication*, «The Bell System Technical Journal», (Vol. 27, pp. 379-423, 623-656).

1.2 N.T.: Between the Surrealist Narrative and the Computer
On the crucial concept of constraint in cybernetics and on its fundamental utility to an organism, see the paper by Ernst Von Glasersfeld (1994), *Cybernetics and the art of living*, «Cybernetics and Systems», 27 (6), pp. 489-497, and the work of Licata cited previously. For the fundamental assumption of an architectural space characterized by the substantial presence of information, see Saggio (2007), particularly in his diction of "informatizzabile space".

1.4 Determinism and Indeterminism: Strategies of Uncertainty
From the surrealist and dada tradition, to action painting, and down to our day, the interest in casual procedures has grown and assumed different meanings. In fact, although related to art, this argument is by nature strictly scientific, and concerns the interest on the part of contemporary science in systems capable of expressing a self-organizational capacity through "casual" interactions. On this, a good synthesis is found in Capra (2005).
It should however be noted that the *random* product of the computer is not at all random. It can be shown, in fact that even behind the apparent randomness, an algorithm works whose results are so predictable that the algorithm itself is called *pseudo-random* (cfr. Von Baeyer 2005).
The concept of *viability* which, together with variability, explains the

behavior of VIAB, seems to be a clear reference to the concept of *viability* in the *embodied* cognition tradition. This latter explains the intimately coherent and systemic nature of the action of organisms in the environment of which they are a part. See also Varela, Thompson, and Rosch (1991).

1.5 The Mind of the Living vs. The Artificial Mind
The useful article by R.D. Coyne (1990), Design Reasoning Without Explanations, «*AI Magazine*», Vol. 11 is useful for a quick framing of the cognitive sciences, Information Technology, and planning processes in architecture. Other research that sheds light on a specialist but lively area are found in J.S. Gero and Z. Bilda (2006), *Reasoning with internal and external representations: A case study with expert architects*, «Proceedings of the Annual Meeting of Cognitive Science Society», R. Sun. (ed), pp. 1020-1026. All of these studies, however, overlook the mental model of psychoanalysis, whereas Roche repeatedly draws upon it in his projects.
Hypnosis and the situationist dérive, two perceptual modes of space in psychoanalysis and situationism, respectively, constitute an openness to mentally unpredictable activities which, in Roche's projects, seem to balance the computational approach so as to avoid deterministic risk. For the concept of the computational mind, characteristic of the classical cognitive sciences, see the complete essay of Piattelli Palmarini (2008).

2. Embedding Information in a Context
In particular, see the work of J. Pallasmaa (2005). In the first part of his text Pallasmaa repeatedly places emphasis on the contemporary condition of the computer elaboration of the project, which is responsible, in his view, for a cold and detached design tendency that emphasizes visual perception at the expense of that haptic, as he states, among others. Pallasmaa's architectural background is in the Nordic tradition. His text recovers the experience of the body by drawing on different thinkers of his own European psychoanalytic tradition, outlining a significant phenomenology of the senses in architecture, but completely neglecting the themes posed by Information Technology.

2.1 Embodiment and Hyper-Localism
For the concept of *embodiment*, common to different aspects of contemporaneous cognitive tradition, see the main texts in the

bibliography relating to the cognitive sciences. However, the prophetic text of Warren McCulloch (1965), *Embodiment of Mind* (MIT Press, Cambridge, MA) should be remembered, as well as the first part of the text of Varela, Thompson, Rosch (1991), and the famous essay of Lakoff, G. and M. Johnson (1999), *Philosophy in the Flesh: The Embodied Mind and Its Challenge to Western Thought* (New York, Basic Books), which is oriented more towards linguistics.

2.2 Protocols of Disappearance
A comprehensive review of the systemic approach and its articulations in contemporary thought is found in Capra (2005).

2.4 The Fine Dust of Information - Order and Disorder
On the thought of Complexity Theory there naturally exists a vast bibliography. For a general introduction on complexity, consult A. Gandolfi (2008), *Formicai, Imperi, Cervelli. Introduzione alla scienza della complessita'* (Torino, Bollati Boringhieri). However we again recommend Licata's text, for its completeness and its ability to unfold the discourse both on the cognitive level as well as on the level of physical systems (Licata 2008). An excellent text that treats the problem from the methodological point of view, with an exploration of the specifics of design processes in architecture, see Paul Coates (2010), *Programming, Architecture* (London, Routledge).

2.5 Disappear - Appear - Detach
The awareness of closed and open ecological systems has a long history that is, on the one hand, intertwined with architecture and, on the other, is owed to the competition in the space race between the USA and the former USSR in the fifties. For a historical study situated between architectural and ecological thought, which is able to clarify many aspects of the question, see P. Anker (2010), *From Bauhaus to Ecohouse, A History of Ecological Design* (USA, Louisiana University Press).

2.6 Ecological Conspiracies Between Architecture and Living Beings
The coupling phenomenology is described in the fundamental work of Maturana and Varela (1985). A more radical view, which also recalls the work of James J. Gibson and his *ecological psychology*, is in Chemero (2009). For a brief profile of Gibson's thought we recommend J. J. Gibson (2002), *A Theory of Direct Visual Perception*,

«Vision and Mind. Selected Readings in the Philosophy of Perception», Noë A. and Thompson E. (ed.) (Cambridge, MIT Press, pp. 85-97).

2.8 Unity Between the Living and Artificial: The Role of the Body
For a look at corporeality as a theme of contemporary thought, and for its relations with machines, a useful essay to add to G. Deleuze's work is that by C. Sini (2009). Sini recovers the instrumental character of the human body in relation to the concepts of the machine and automation, and examines the philosophical ideas of greatest relevance to information.

2.9 Elephants Don't Play Chess
Elephants Don't Play Chess (Brooks 1990), which gives the title to this paragraph, is the direct citation of the title of a well-known article by the robot expert Rodney A. Brooks. The article marks the transition in robotics, and more generally in the studies of artificial intelligence, from a concept of the mind similar to the computer as we know it, to that in which the mind, to function, must be located within a body and a context.
The concept that Brooks proposes is that of *the cognitive architecture of subsumption* (Brooks 1990), where different levels of knowledge are subsumed into one another, beginning from the most elementary levels of physical interaction, and proceeding to those more complex where intelligent behavior on the part of an artificial agent is the result of different circumstances which are not exclusively identified in a computational treatment of information.

2.10 ... But Robots, Yes (Do Play Chess)!
The stochastic algorithm, such as that used in the Olzweg robot, is based on the model of *Brownian motion*, which permit it to configure steps of uncertain branching in the very development of the phenomenon. This approach is more probabilistic than deterministic, which in the case in question allows the particular evolution of the addition planned for the museum. Olzweg is also a term that clearly refers to Heidegger's *Holzwege* (1950), or rather to the *broken paths* and the *erratic thought*.

2.11 And the Body?
For a general discussion on the relationship between body and architecture, refer to the extensive and varied collection of essays

edited by G. Dodds and R. Tavernor (2005), *Body and Building: Essays on the Changing Relation of a Body and Architecture* (Cambridge, MA, MIT Press). A critical summary closer to the themes of Information Technology is in K. Jormakka (2005), *Genius Locomotionis* (Vienna, ed. Selene). M. Palumbo's text, published in this book series, is relevant along the same lines. See M. L. Palumbo (2001), *Nuovi Ventri. Corpi elettronici e disordini architettonici* (Torino, Testo&Immagine).

2.12 Co-evolution Between Architecture and the Environment
The concept of co-evolution as a cognitive engine of organisms in an environment is particularly present in the work of Varela, Thompson, and Rosch (1991). For the concept of mutualistic symbiosis, and in particular of *endosymbiosis*, consult the work of the American biologist Lynn Margulis, well-documented in Capra (2005). Margulis, who died recently, is known in scientific circles for his research on the evolution of life on Earth, designed to emphasize the role of collaboration and interconnection between systems more than competition.

2.13 In Symbiosis with the Cosmos: Hyper-Architectural Research
For two antithetical but complementary visions in the history of cybernetics, the result of various personalities such as N. Wiener, J. Von Neumann, and W. McCulloch, consult especially the first part of the work of Licata (2008).

2.14 Constructive and Destructive Architectural Machines
The ability to not only generate but also destroy its own components, in order to continuously produce itself, is what distinguishes an *autopoietic* machine from an *allopoietic* one (the latter being a machine capable only of producing something else). The distinction is the basis of the known *phenomenology of the living* of Maturana and Varela (1985).

3. Towards an Architecture as a Living System
Different critical positions of many visions emphasize an ever more intimate relationship between architecture and biological systems, but not always with the proper precautions.
Given the vastness of the topic I think it is worth mentioning the first architecture to raise the issue of the living, the result of the pioneering

work of the *Biosphere 2* project. Some articles that investigate this matter are: J. Allen, Al, W. Dempster, M. Nelson, S. Silverstone, and M. Van Thillo (2005), *Lessons Learned from Biosphere 2 and Laboratory Biosphere Closed Systems. Experiments for the Mars on Earth © Project*, «Biological Sciences in Space» (Vol. 19, No. 4, pp. 250-260), and the fundamental J.P. Allen, M. Nelson, and A. Alling (2003), *The Legacy of Biosphere 2 for the Study of Biospherics and closed ecological Systems*, «A & Space Res » (Vol. 31, No. 7, pp. 1629-1639, Great Britain, Elsevier Science).

Long-forgotten and eclipsed by desire, perhaps due to the competition of certain American scientific circles, the project clearly poses the problem of the realization of an architecture able to work in tandem with living systems.

This is accomplished through a setting attributed to cybernetics, to synergism, and more generally to the desire to create a *Galilean experiment* able to organize a closed ecological system with regard to the exchanges of energy and information. This was an unbelievable attempt to create a reproduction of the Terrestrial Biosphere, from which the project also derived its name *Biosphere 2.*

3.1 The Project of New-Territories as a Strategy for Living Architecture

The purpose of a living system for Maturana and Varela is nothing other than the continued production of the self. Such a cryptic statement might not be understood if one does not continue in the wake of the two to discover that such a continuous production of the self is just cognition. Knowledge is thus entered into the domain of biology; information is in the organization of the system.

3.2 An Architecture that is Self-Produced

N.T. seems to be the first group of architects to propose, through the use of robots, a plausible strategy for the production and destruction of components of an architecture. They propose a transformative logic based on the regeneration of the components themselves.

The concept of *autopoiesis* is thus explained by Maturana and Varela (1985): *an autopoietic machine is a machine organized (defined as a unit) as a network of processes of production (transformation and destruction) that produces components which: I) through their continuous interactions and transformations regenerate and realize the network of processes (relations) that produce them; and II) constitute it (the machine) as a concrete unity in the space in which they (the components) exist by specifying the topological domain of its realization in that network* (p. 131).

3.3 Information, Energy, and Matter

For a reflection on information under a strictly scientific and enlightening profile with regard to its relations with other sciences, see the book of Von Baeyer (2005).

Summary

Living Architectures: Heresy or Future?   5
preface by Antonino Saggio

1. A Critical Position: Reconcilable Dualities Between Machines
   and Living Entities   11
Preamble - Aqua Alta in Venice   11
1.1. New-Territories.com: New Territories for Heretical Scenarios   13
1.2 N.T.: Between the Surrealist Narrative and the Computer   14
1.3 I've heard about   17
1.4 Determinism and Indeterminism, Strategies of Uncertainty   23
1.5 The Mind of the Living vs. The Artificial Mind   25

2. Embedding Information in a Context   28
2.1 Embodiment and Hyper-Localism   28
2.2 Protocols of Disappearance   33
2.3 ...Or of Apparition?   38
2.4 The Fine Dust of Information - Order and Disorder   44
2.5 Disappear - Appear - Detach   47
2.6 Ecological Conspiracies Between Architecture and Living Beings   47
2.7 Against Memory and for Re-Creation   50
2.8 Unity Between the Living and Artificial: The Role of the Body   54
2.9 Elephants Don't Play Chess   55
2.10 ...But Robots, Yes (Do Play Chess)!   57
2.11 And the Body?   61
2.12 Co-evolution Between Architecture and the Environment   64
2.13 In Symbiosis with the Cosmos: Hyper-Architectural Research   65
2.14 Constructive and Destructive Architectural Machines   70

3. Towards an Architecture as a Living System   73
*3.1 The Project of New-Territories as a Strategy
   for Living Architecture*   73
3.2 An Architecture that is Self-Produced   74
3.3 Information, Energy, Matter   74

Gre(Y)en *by François Roche*   75

Bibliography and Further Reading   85

The Information Technology Revolution in Architecture is a series reflecting on the effects the virtual dimension is having on architects and architecture in general. Each volume will examine a single topic, highlighting the essential aspects and exploring their relevance for the architects of today.

Series edited by **Antonino Saggio**

Other titles in this series

Diller + Scofidio
Il teatro
della dissolvenza
Antonello Marotta
ISBN 88-7864-010-7 *italiano*
ISBN 978-1-4466-7679-0 *inglese*

Gamezone
Playground tra scenari virtuali
e realtà
Alberto Iacovoni
ISBN 88-7864-011-5 *italiano*
ISBN 978-3764301514 *inglese*

Strati Mobili
Video contestuali
nell'Arte e nell'Architettura
Alexandro Ladaga & Silvia Manteiga
ISBN 88-7864-016-6 *italiano*
ISBN 978-1-291-46309-5 *inglese*

Takis Zenetos
Visioni digitali,
architetture costruite
Dimitris Papalexopoulos, Eleni Kalafati
ISBN 88-7864-012-3

Arie italiane
Motivi dell'architettura
italiana recente
Antonello Marotta, Paola Ruotolo
ISBN 88-7864-022-0

Stanze ribelli
Immaginando
lo spazio hacker
Alexander Levi, Amanda Schachter
ISBN 978-88-7864-028-3

Penezic & Rogina
Digitalizzazione
della realtà
Nigel Whiteley
ISBN 978-88-7864-030-6 *italiano*
ISBN 978-1-4461-0015-8 *inglese*

Ipercorpi
Verso una
architettura e-motiva
Kas Oosterhuis
ISBN 978-88-7864-037-5 *italiano*
ISBN 978-37664369699 *inglese*

Ito digitale
Nuovi media,
nuovo reale
Patrizia Mello
ISBN 978-88-7864-044-3

SHoP Works
Collaborazioni costruttive
in digitale
Stefano Converso
ISBN 978-88-7864-045-0 *italiano*
ISBN 978-1-4478-4748-9 *inglese*

Cyberstone
Innovazioni digitali
sulla pietra
Christian R. Pongratz, M. Rita Perbellini
ISBN 978-88-7864-051-4

La forma come memoria
Una teoria geometrica
dell'architettura
Michael Leyton
ISBN 978-88-7864-055-9 *italiano*
ISBN 978-3764376901 *inglese*

Van Berkel digitale
Diagrammi, processi, modelli
di UNStudio
Andrea Sollazzo
ISBN 978-88-7864-070-2 *italiano*
ISBN 978-1-4478-6706-7 *inglese*

Smart Creatures
Progettazione parametrica
per architetture sostenibili
Cesare Griffa
ISBN 978-88-7864-091-7

Plasma Works
Dalle geometrie topologiche
al landscape urbanism
Maria Elisabetta Bonafede
ISBN 978-88-7864-093-1

François Roche
Eresie macchiniche e architetture viventi di
New-Territories.com
Antonino Di Raimo
ISBN 978-88-7864-102-0 *italiano*
ISBN 978-1-291-88380-0 *inglese*

Printed in Great Britain
by Amazon